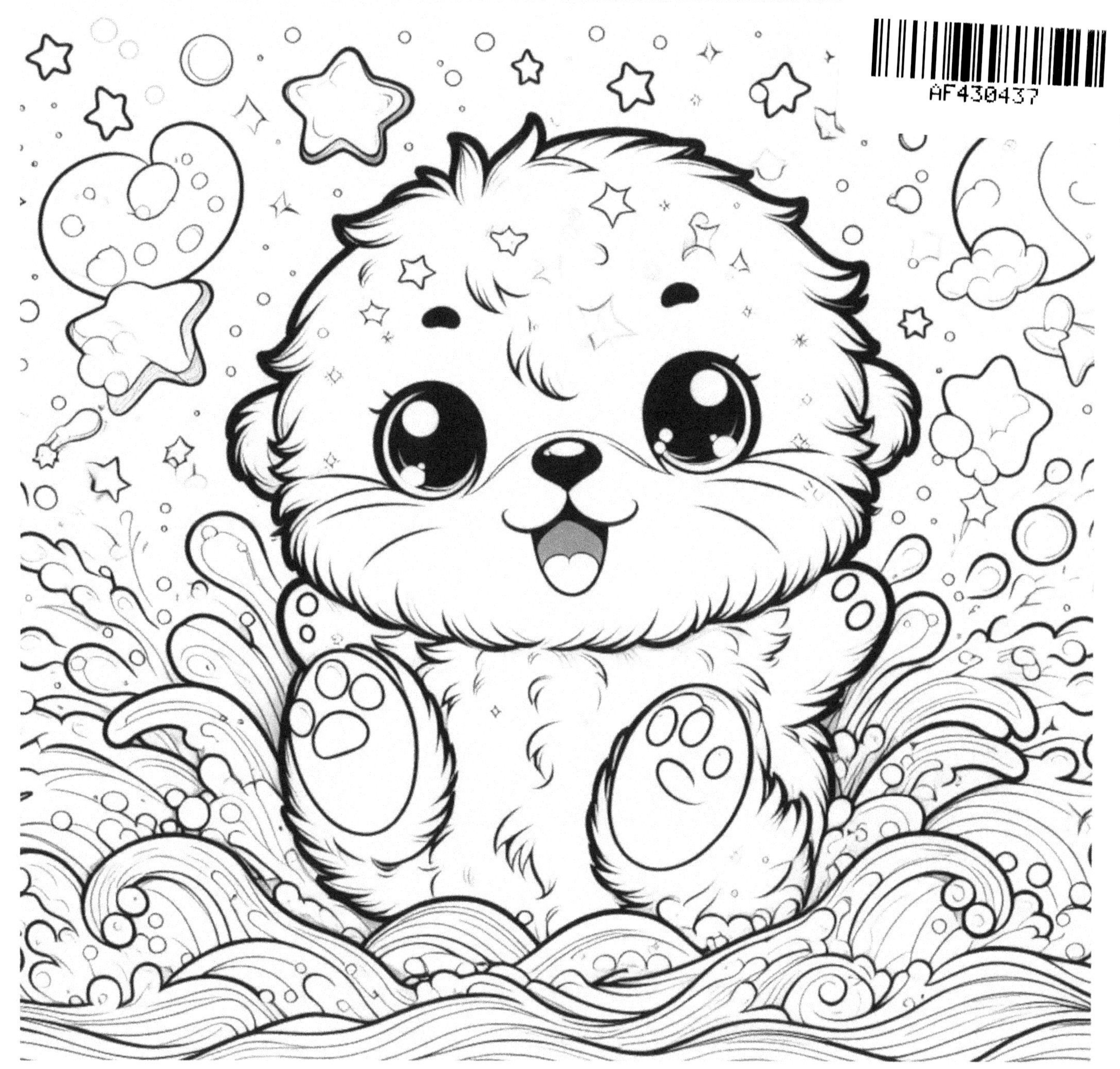

Copyright © 2024

Illustrator - Creative Designer: Valentina VAROL

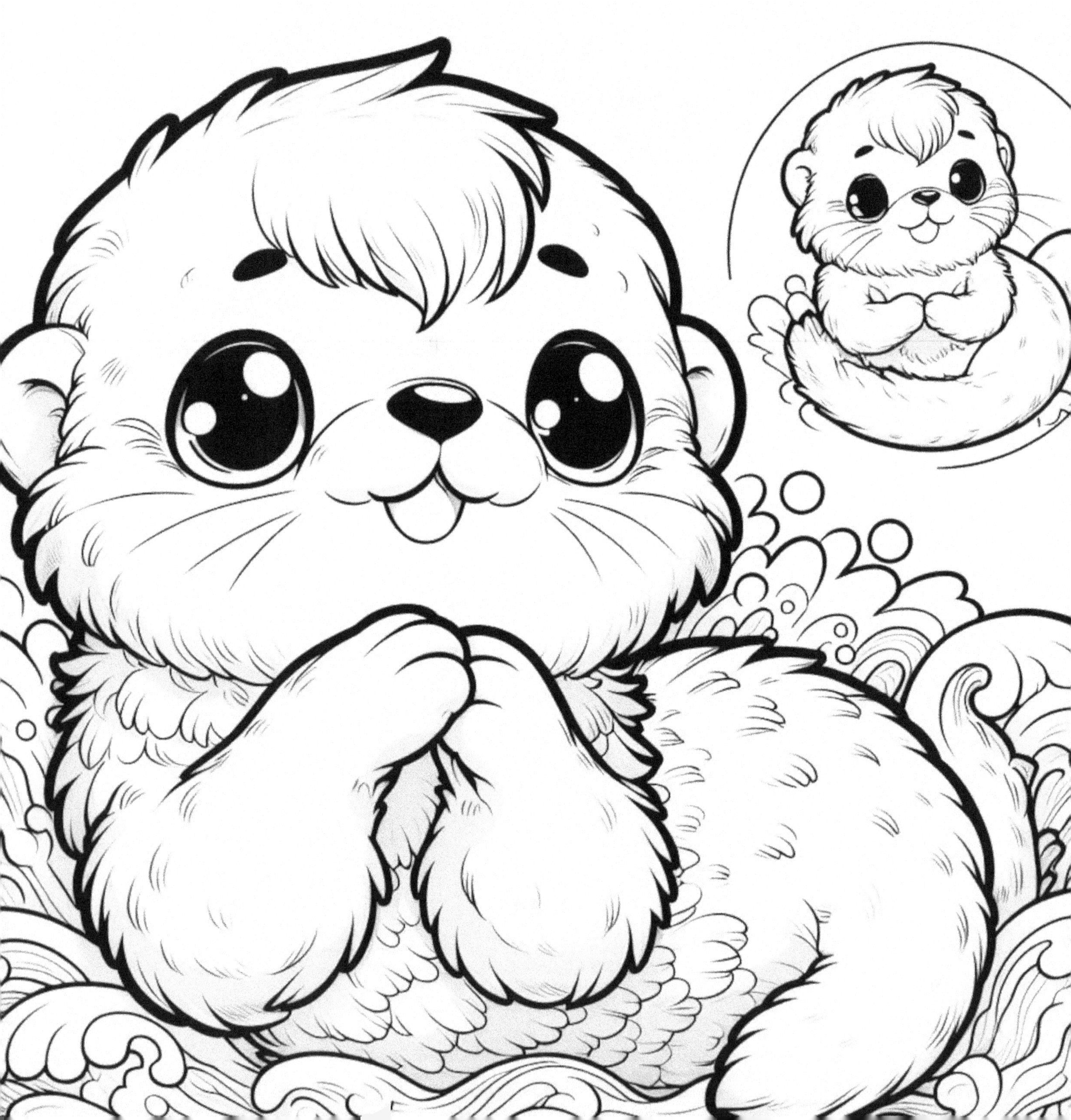

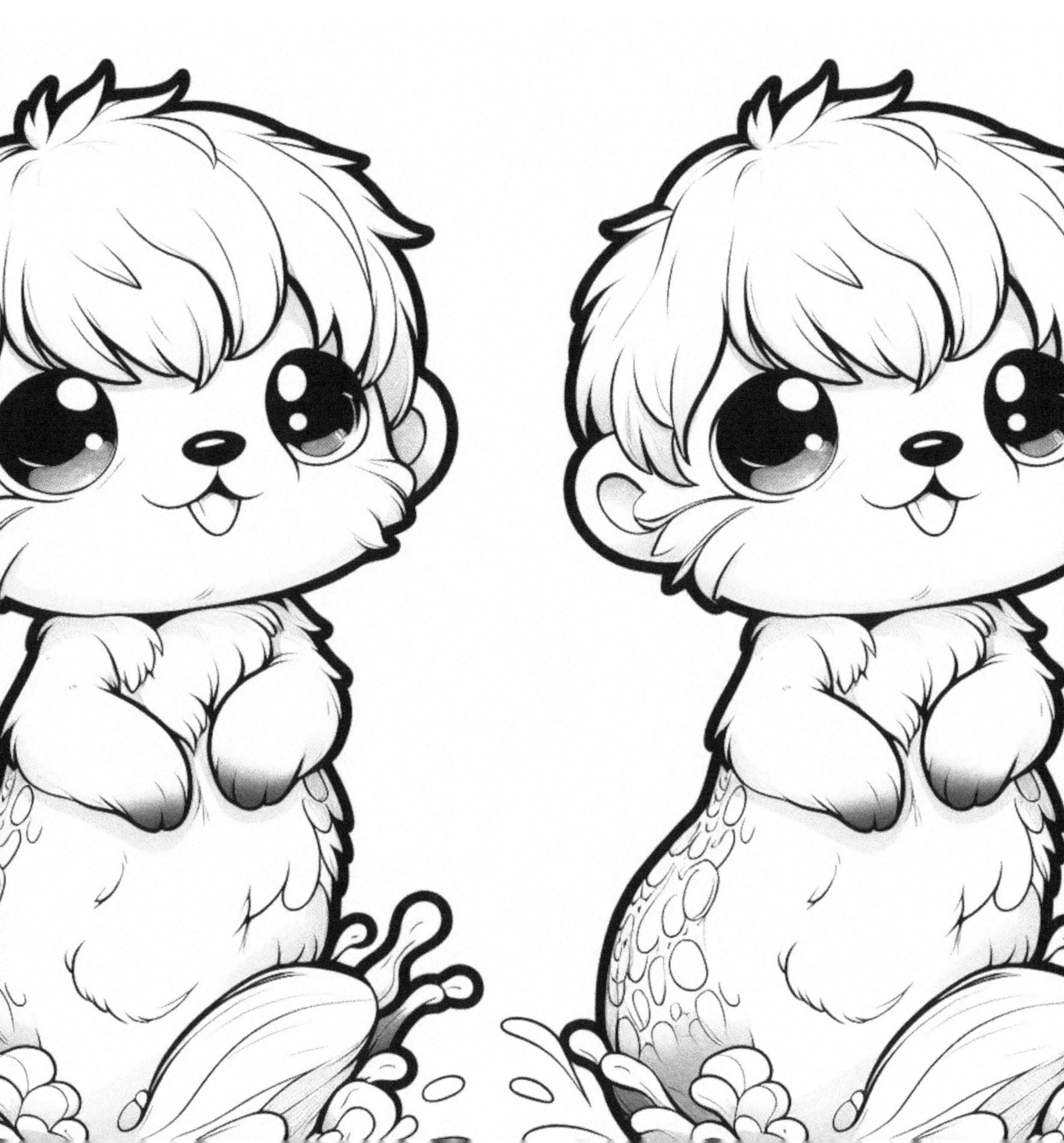

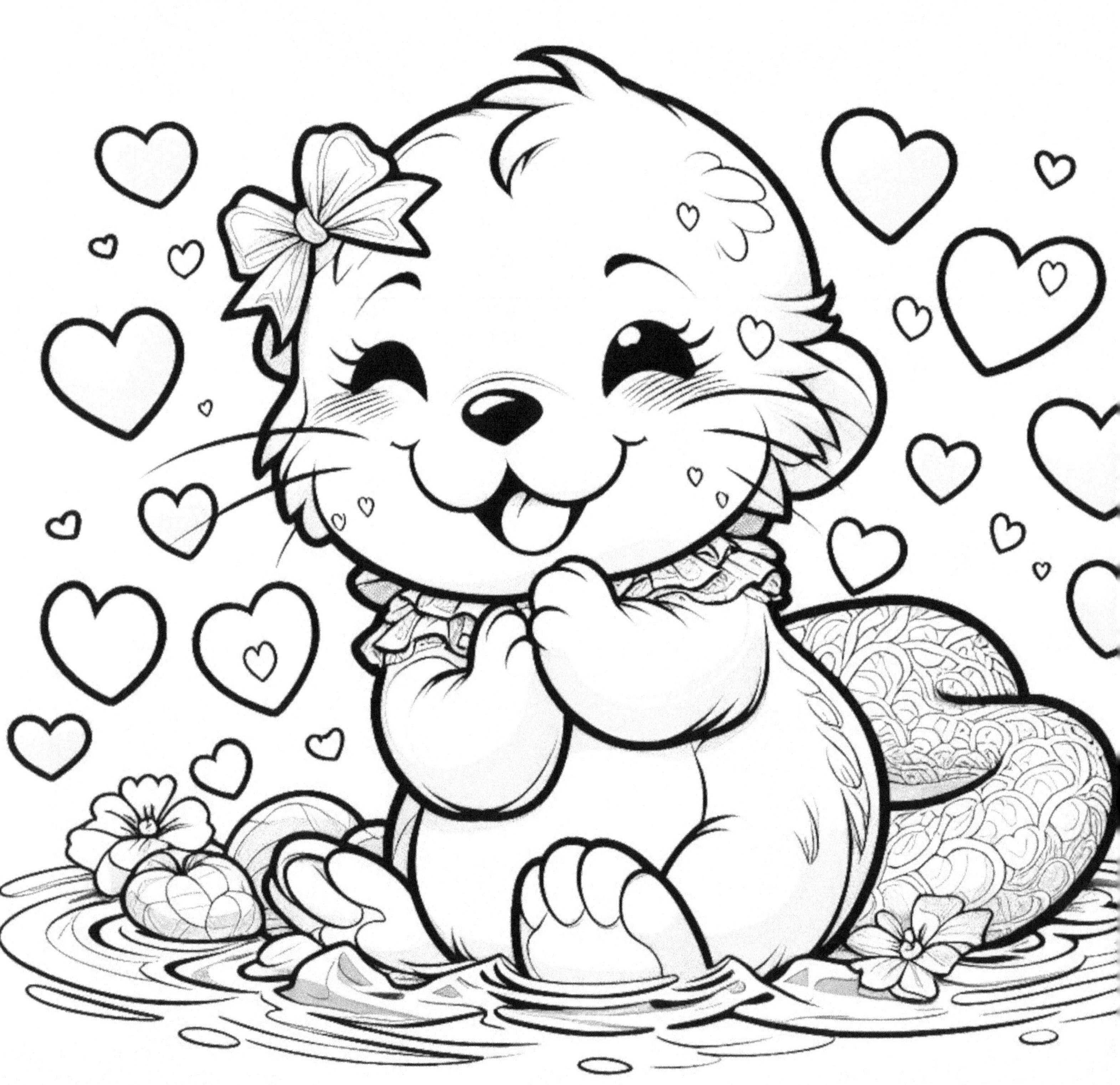

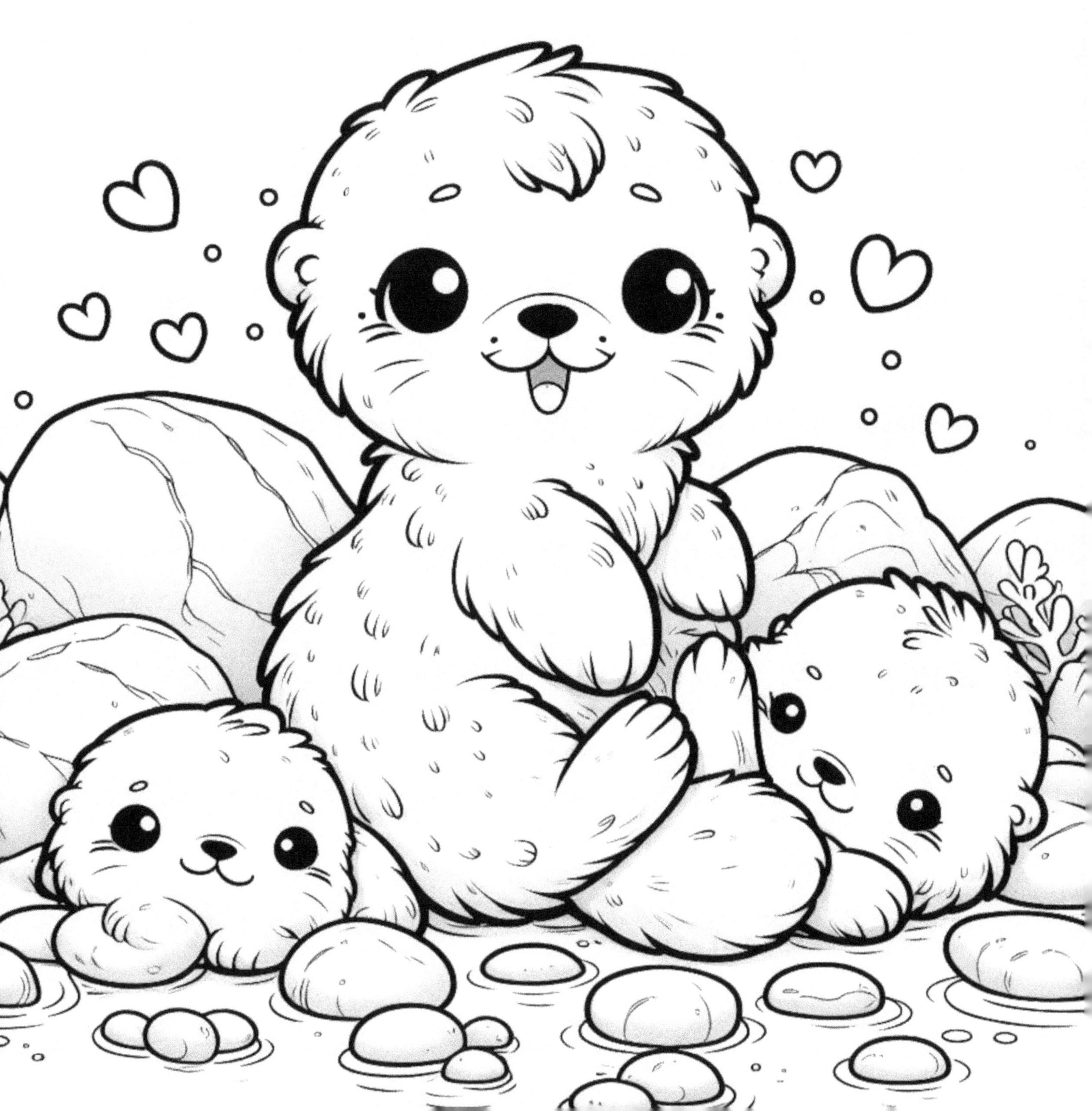

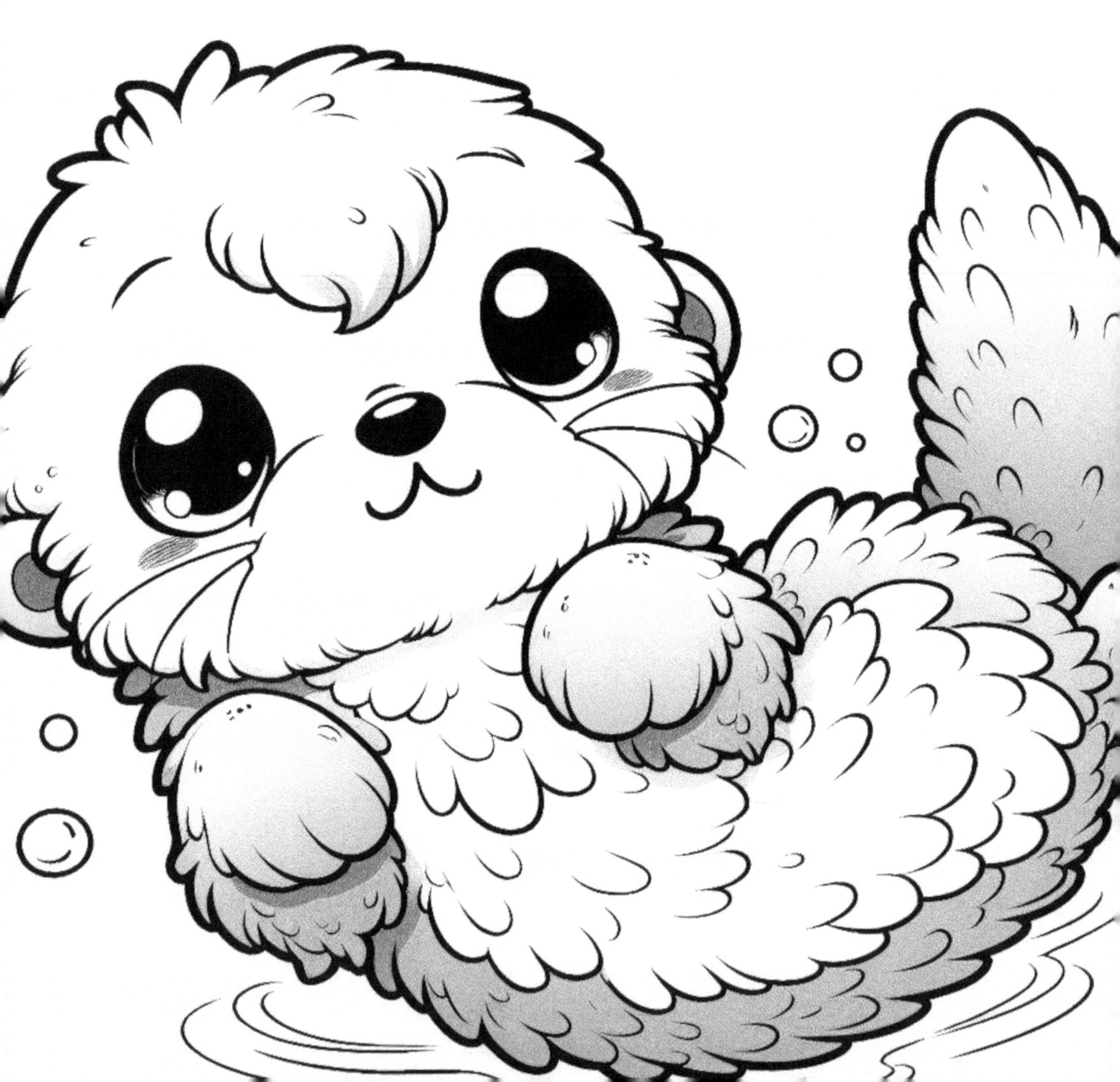

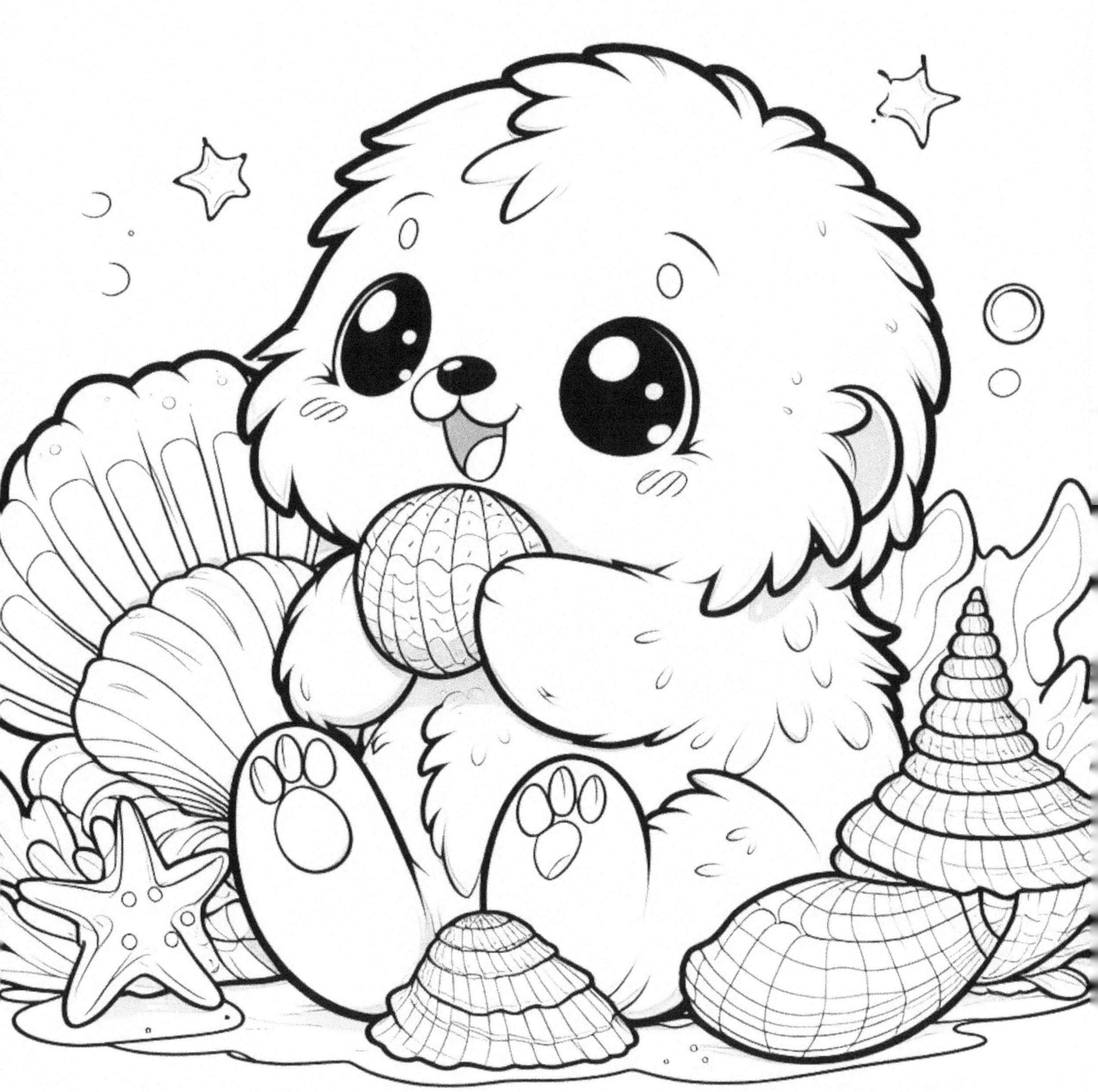

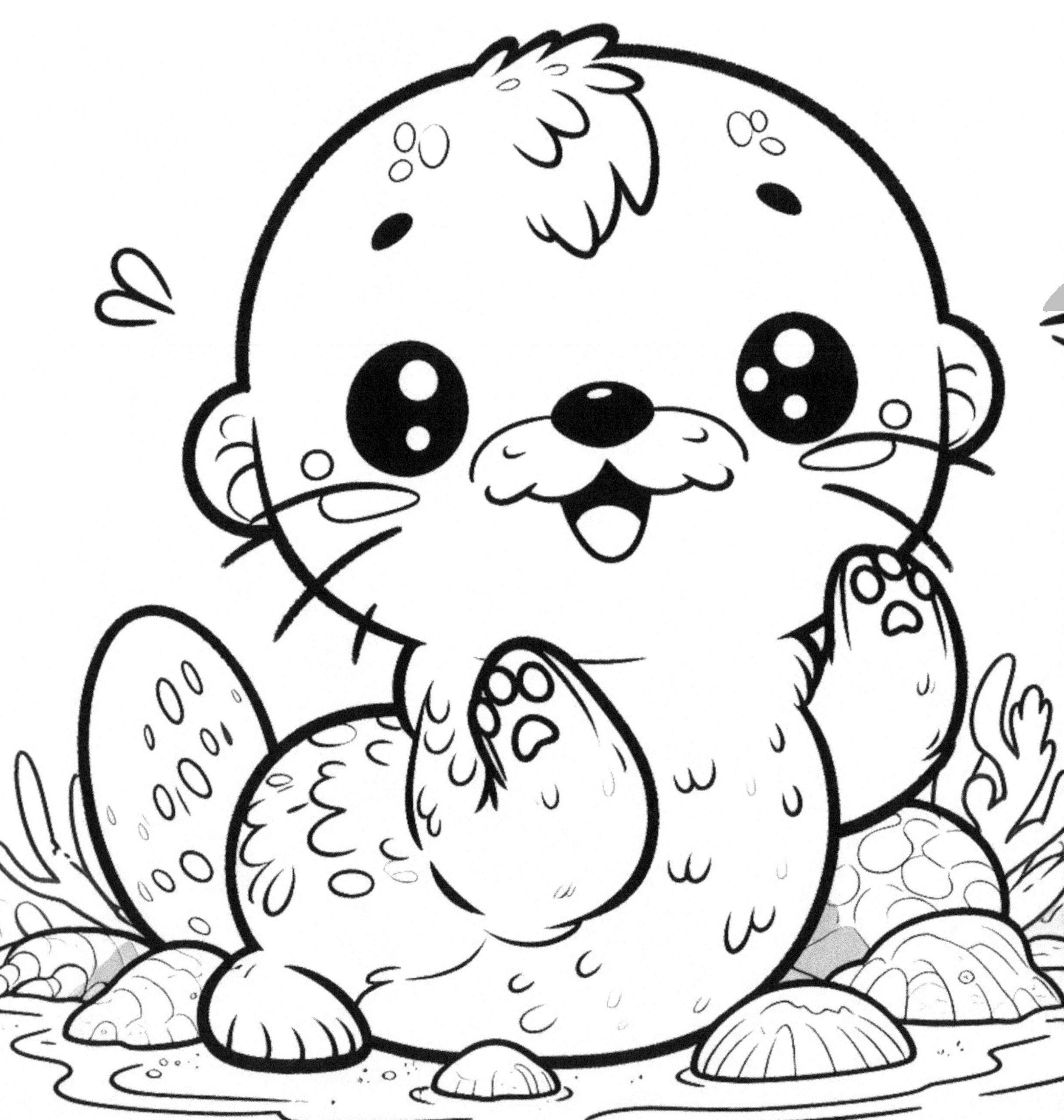

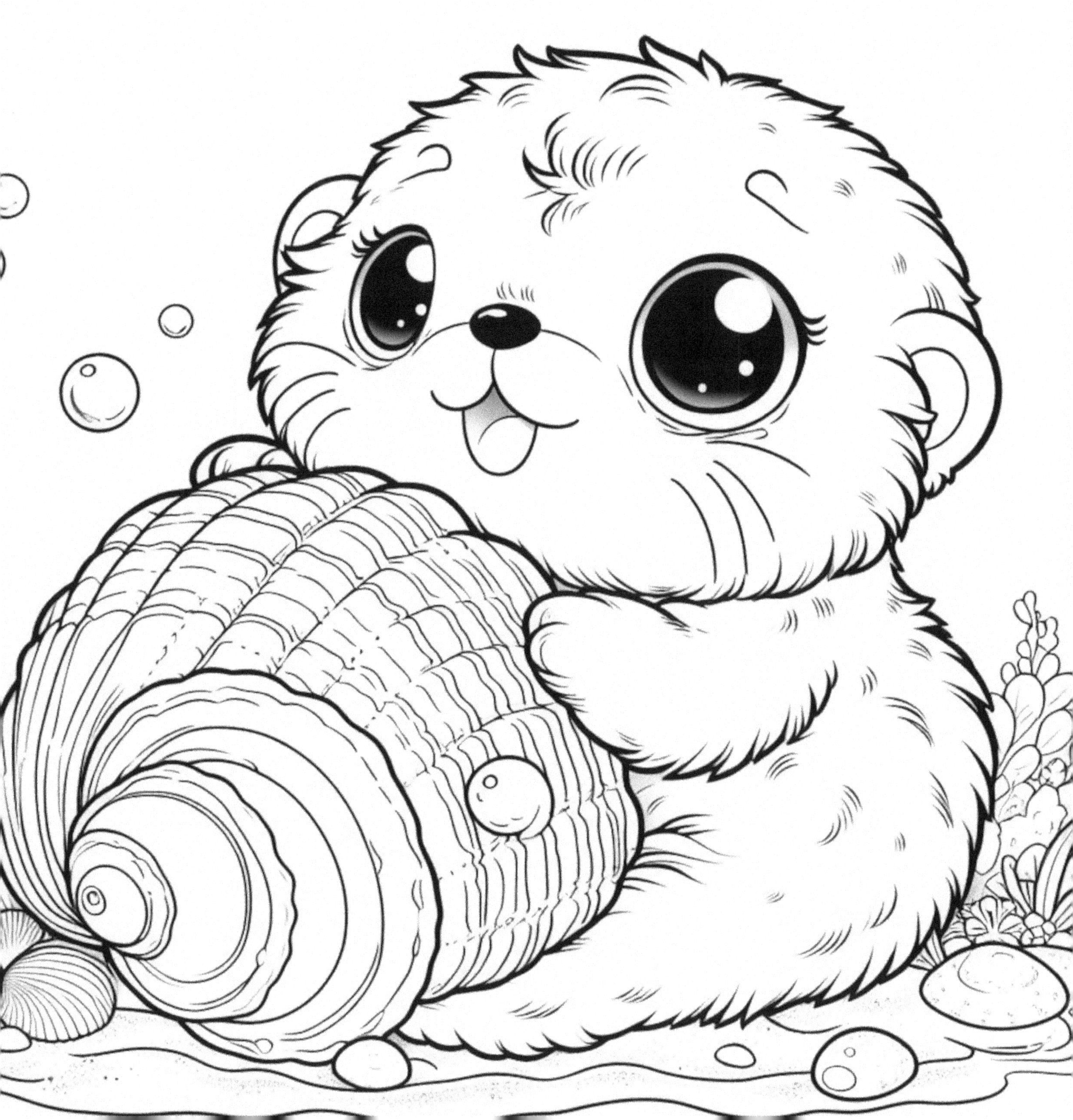

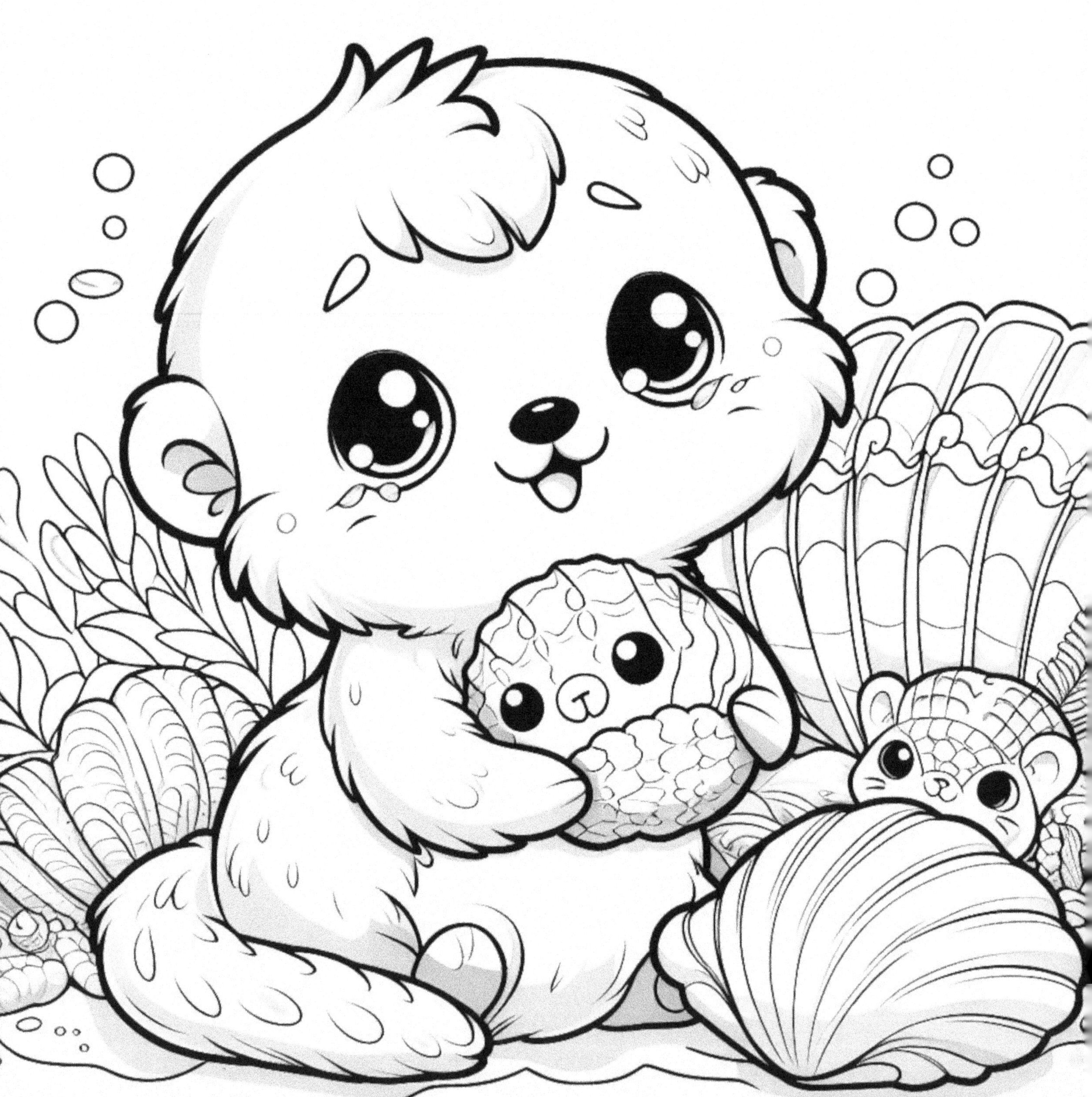

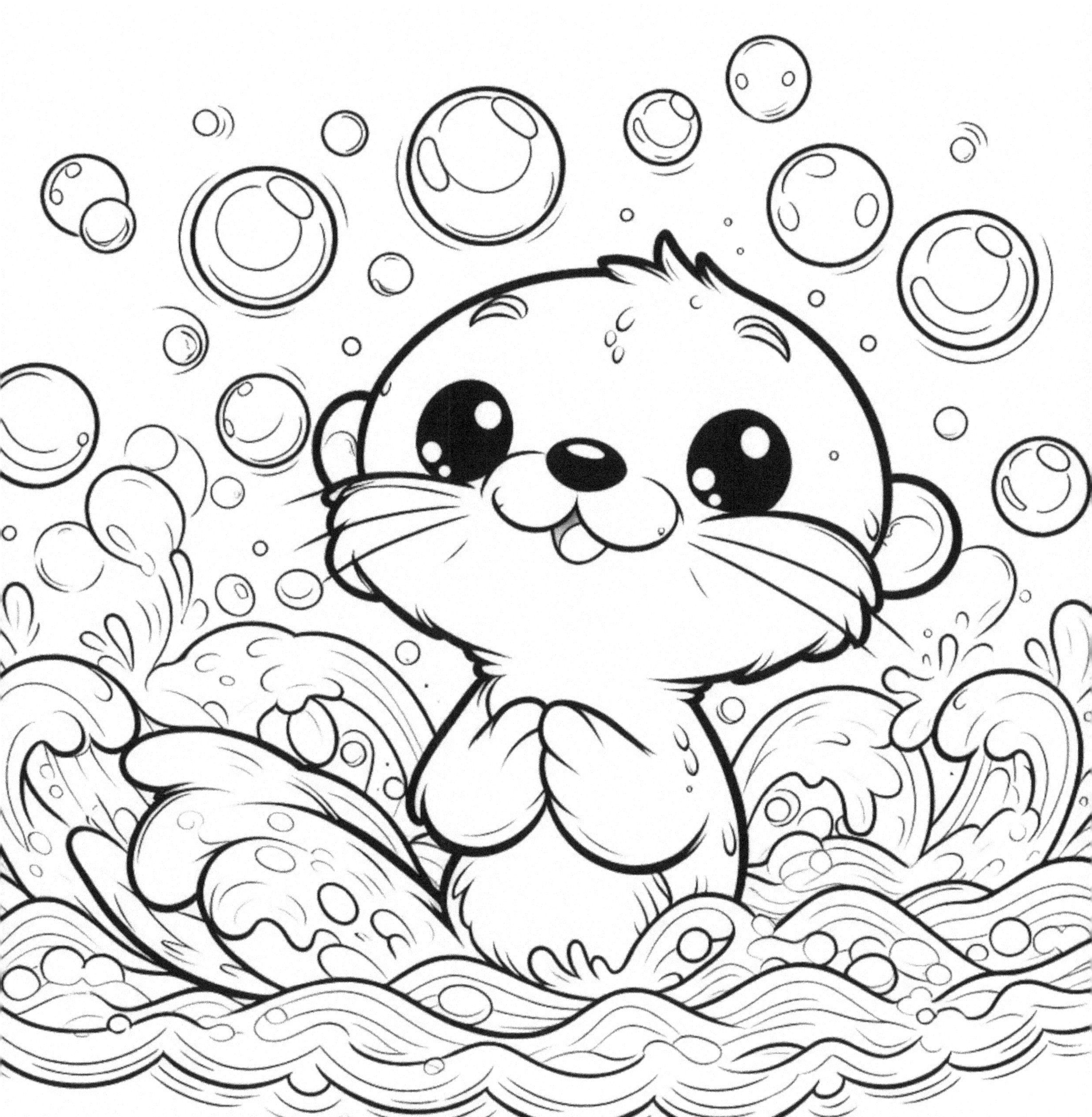

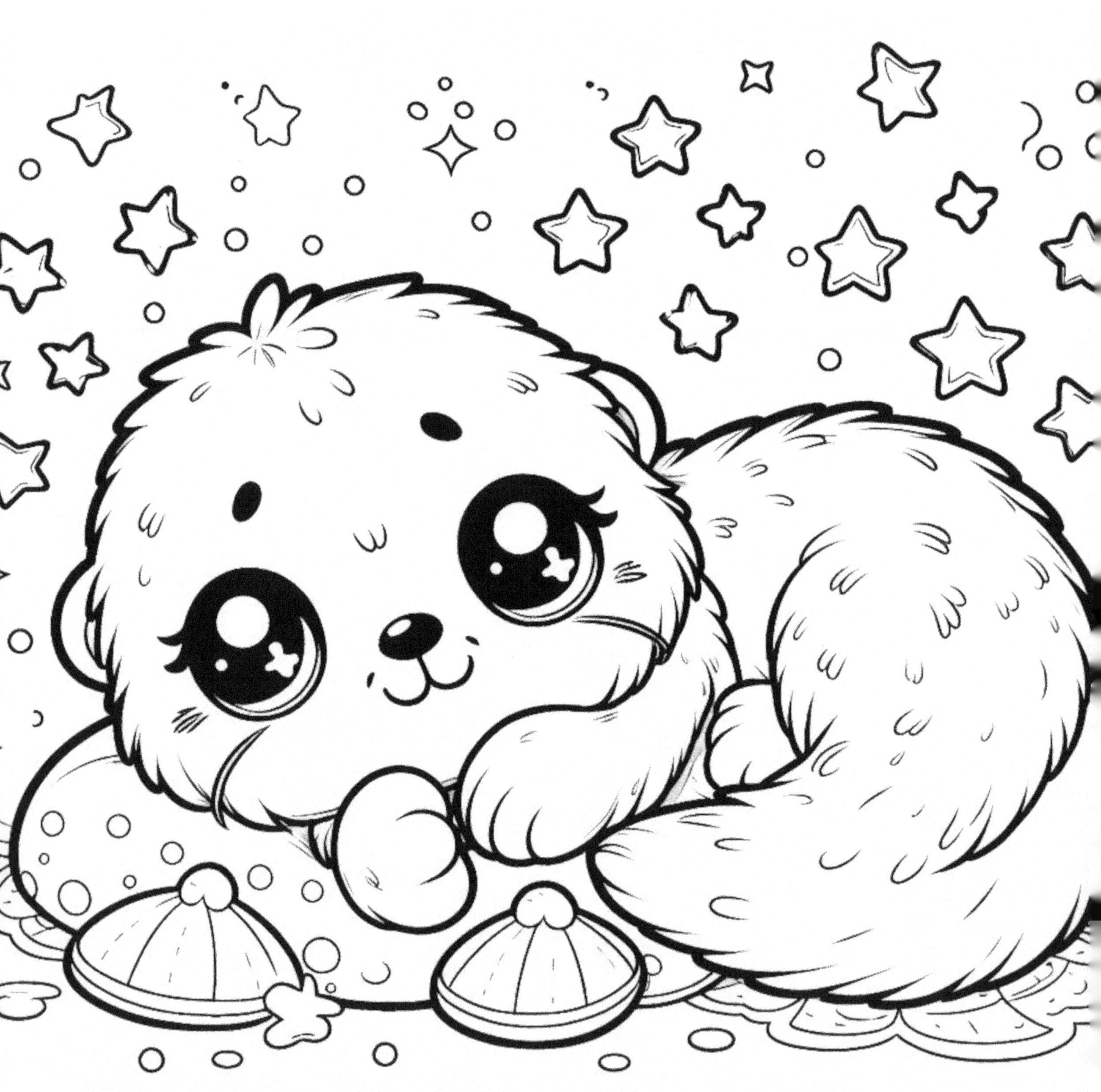

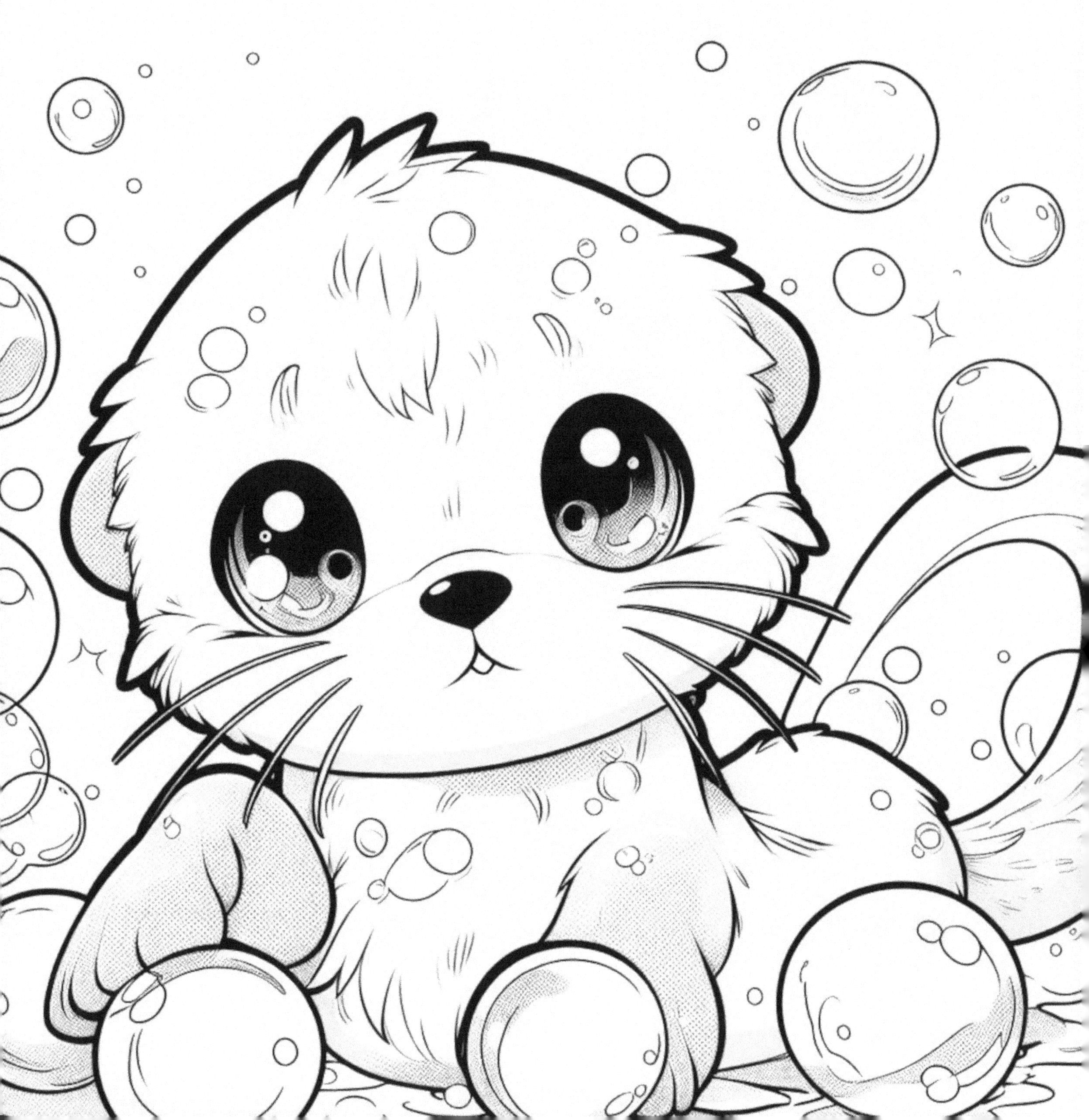

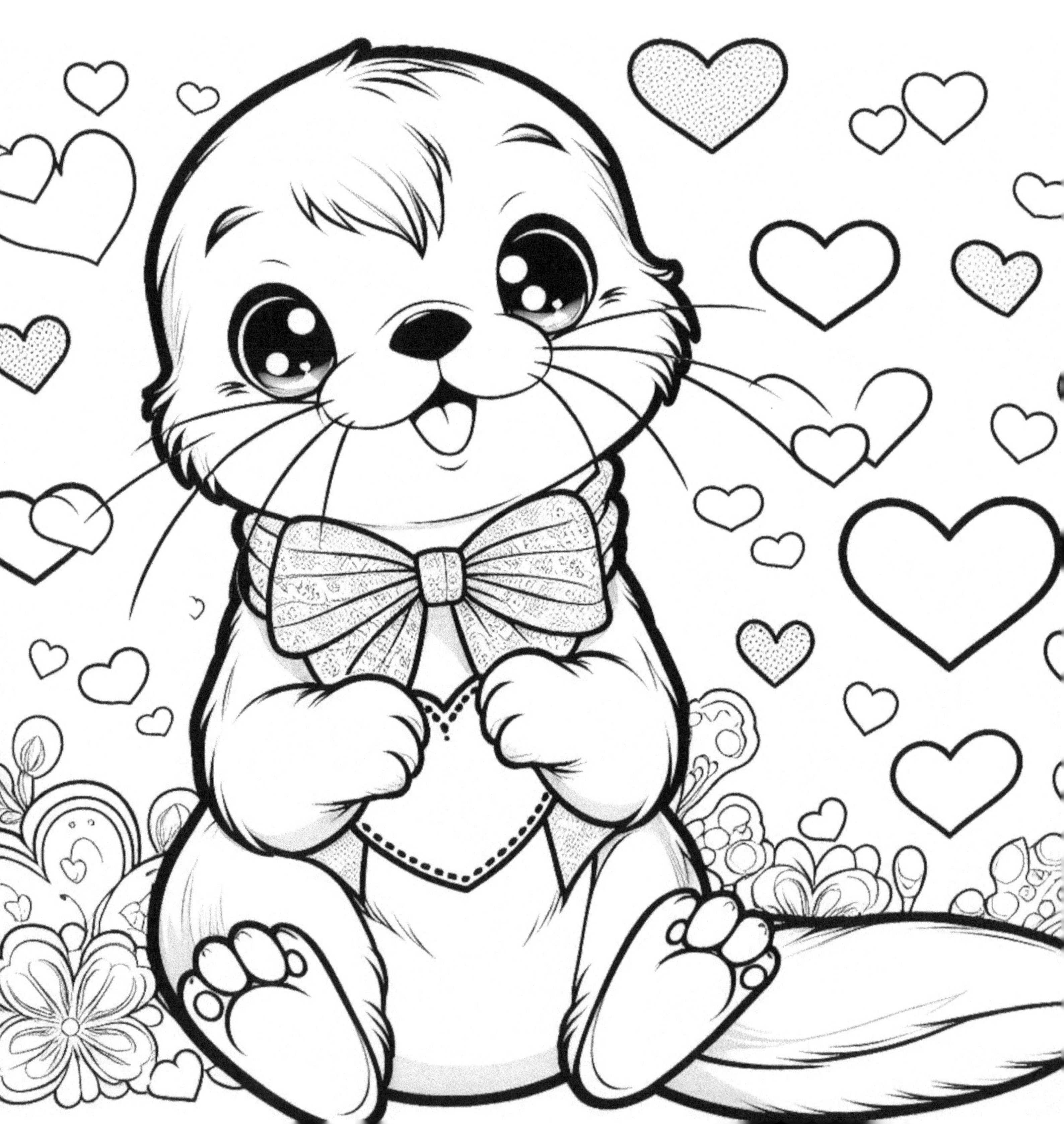

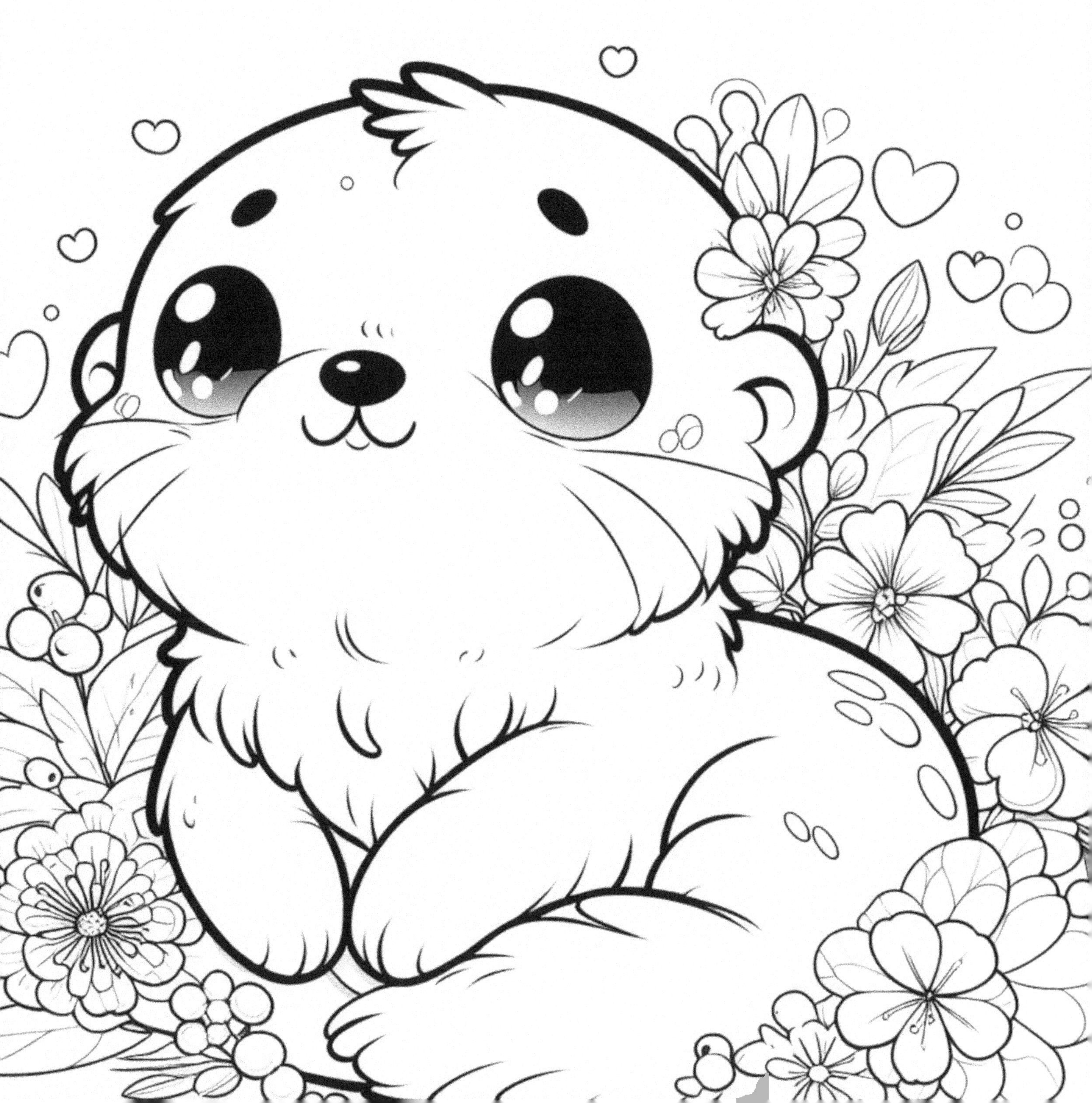

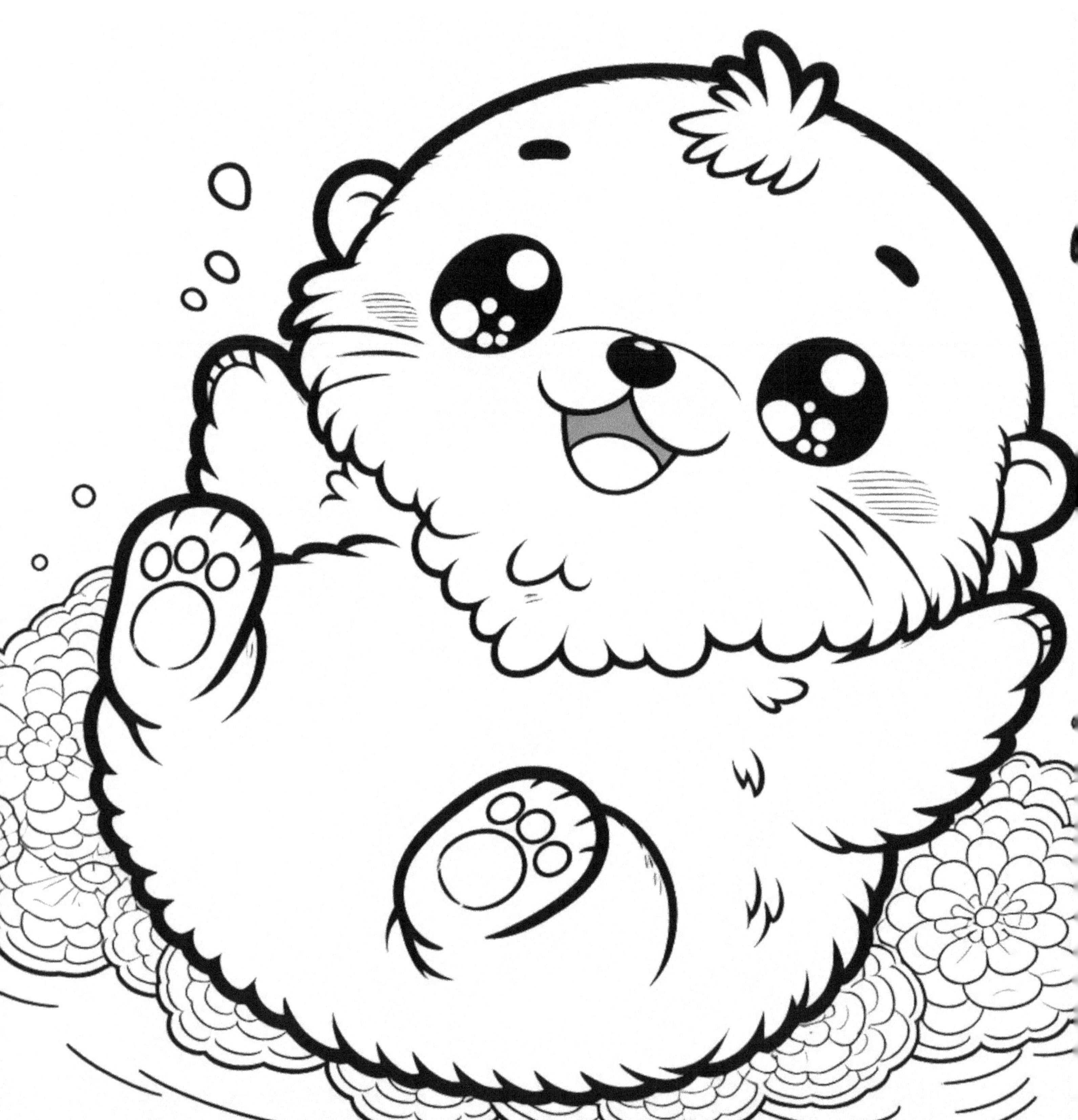

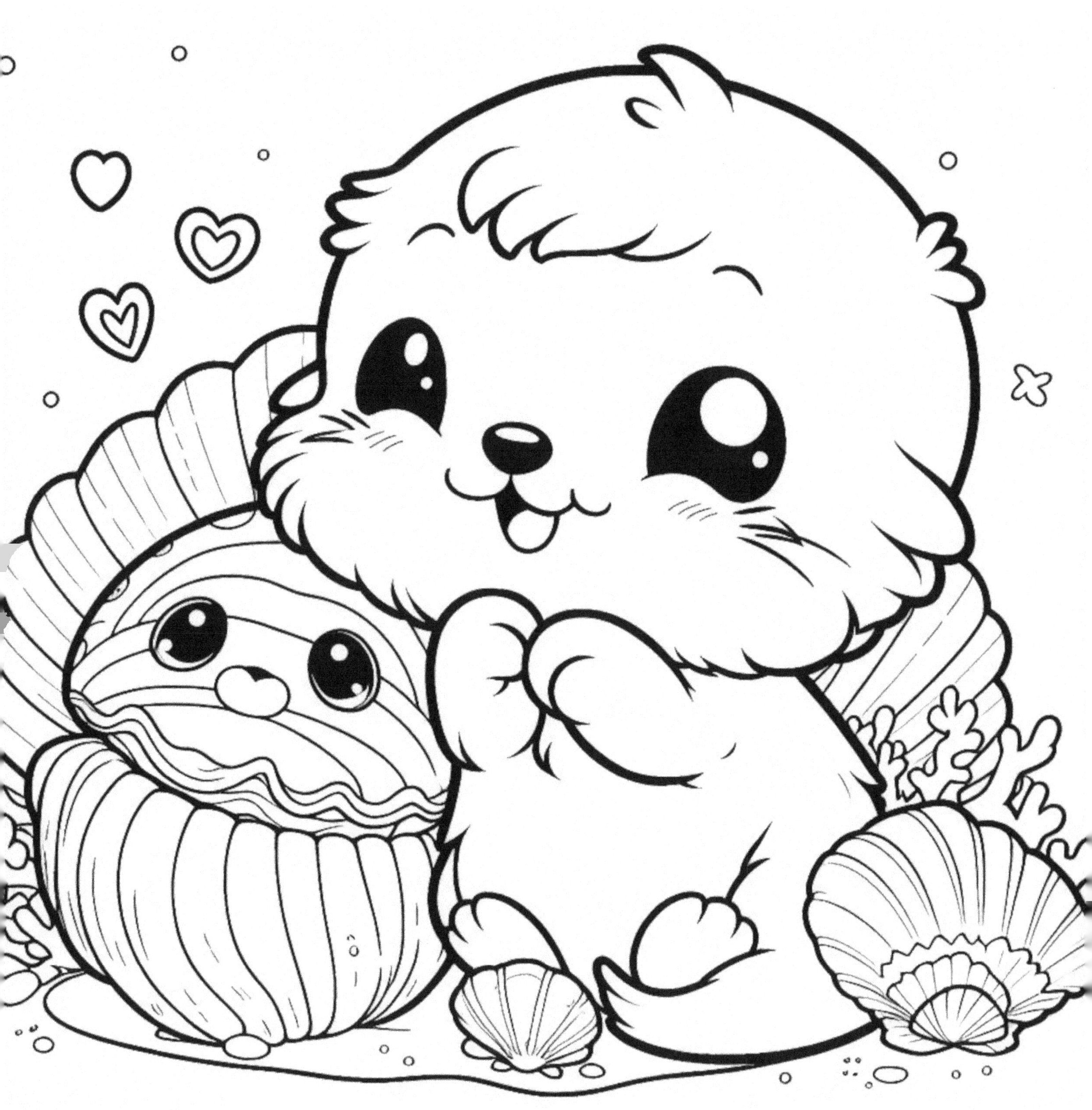

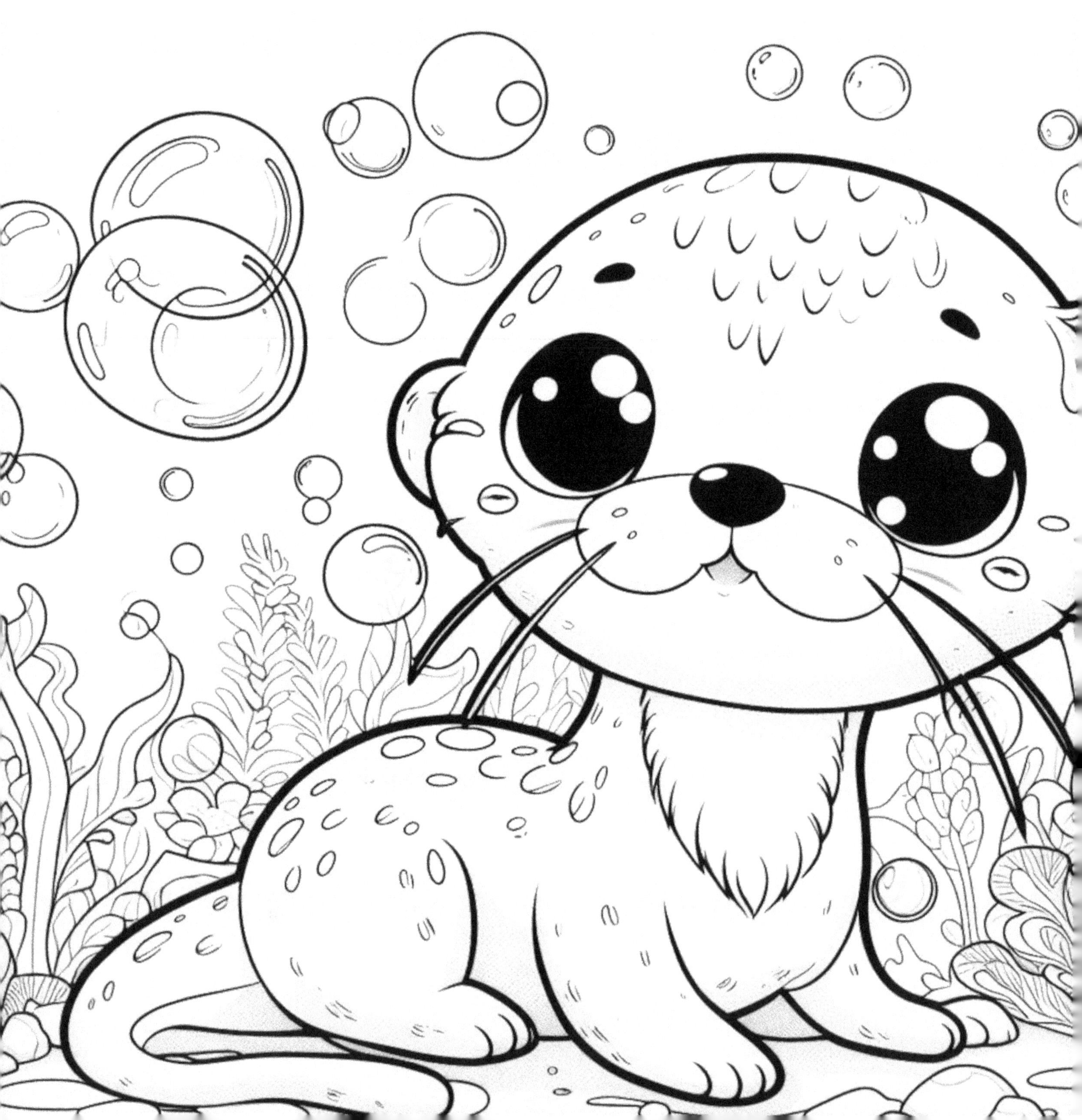

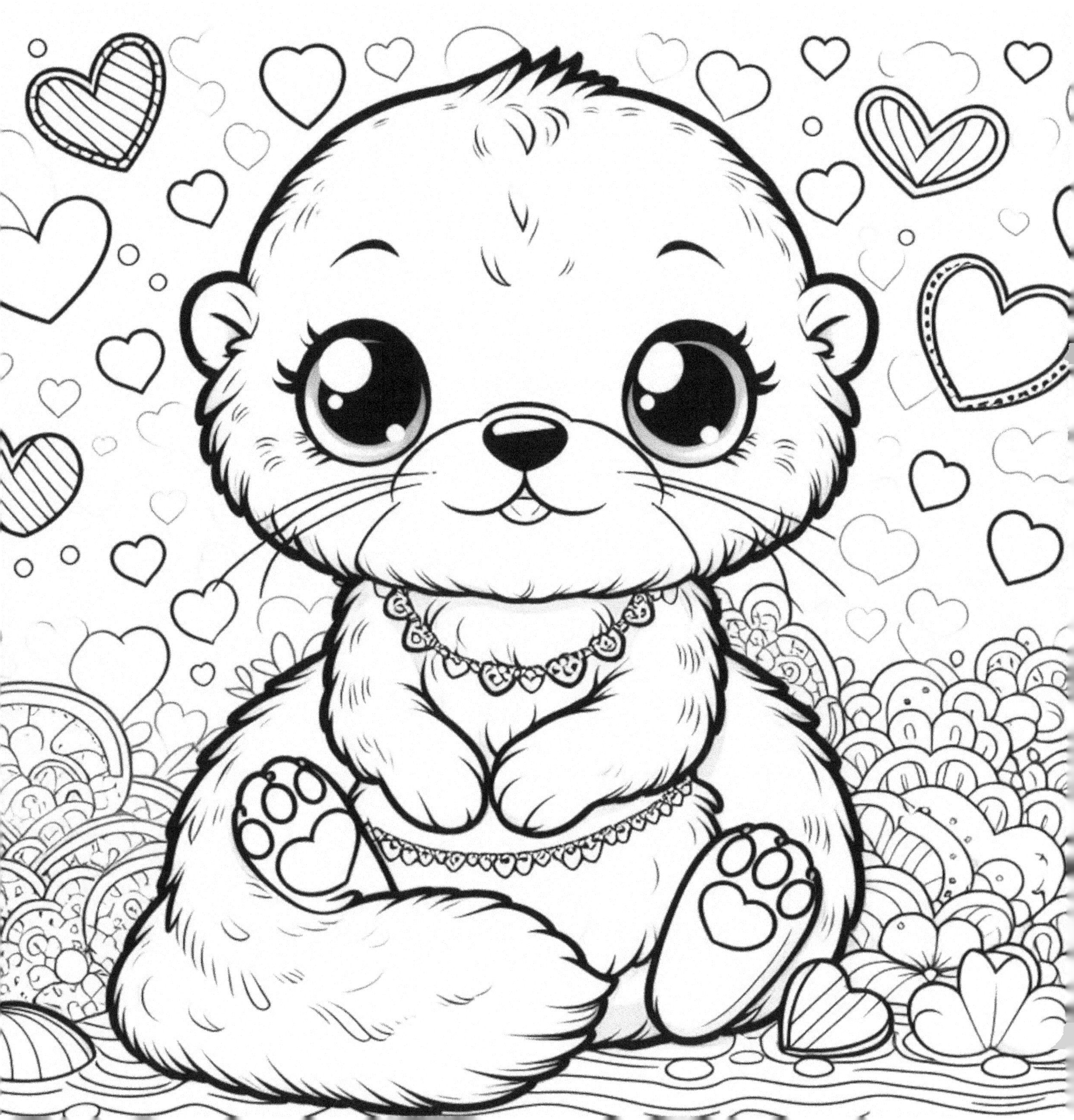

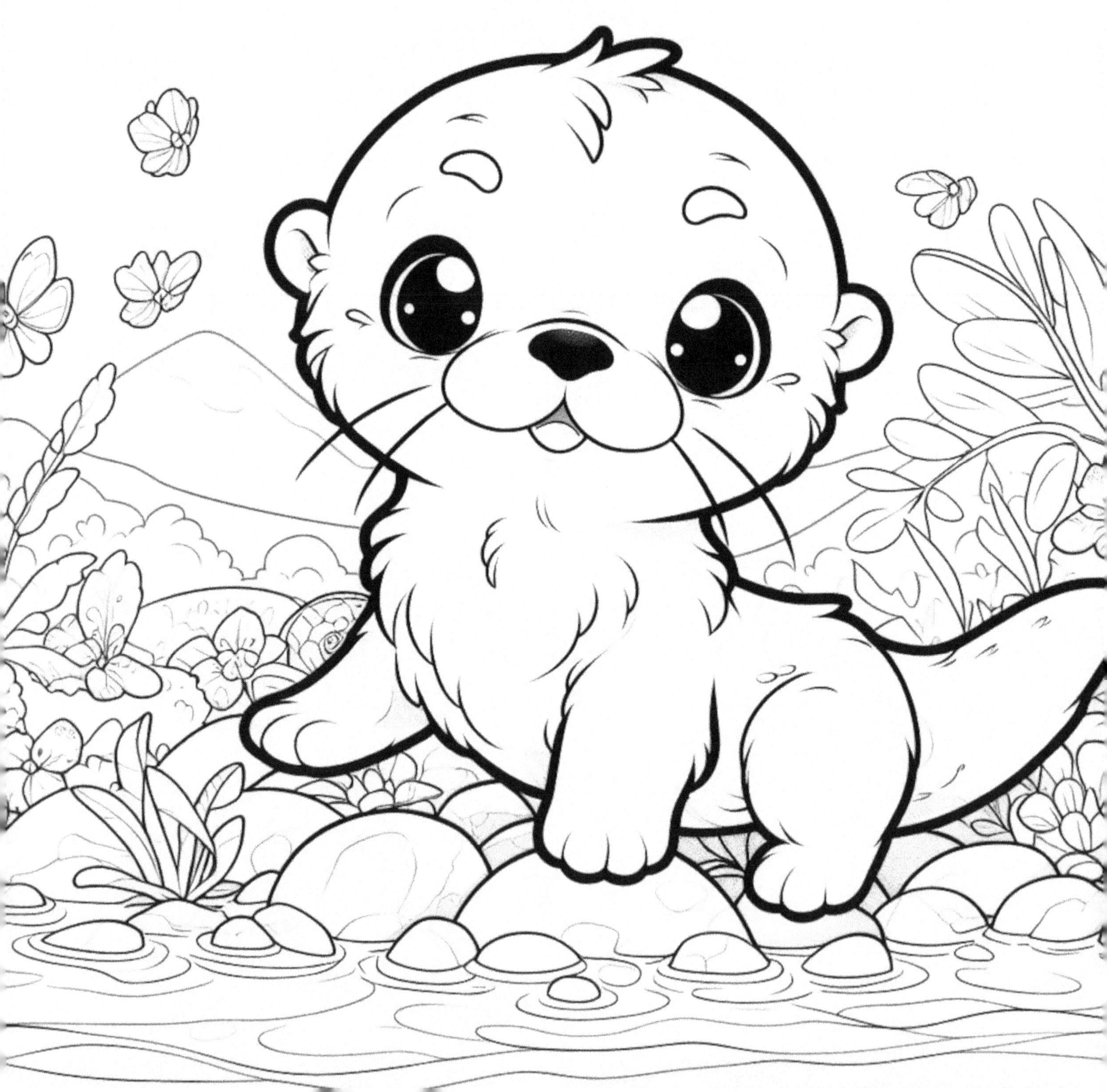

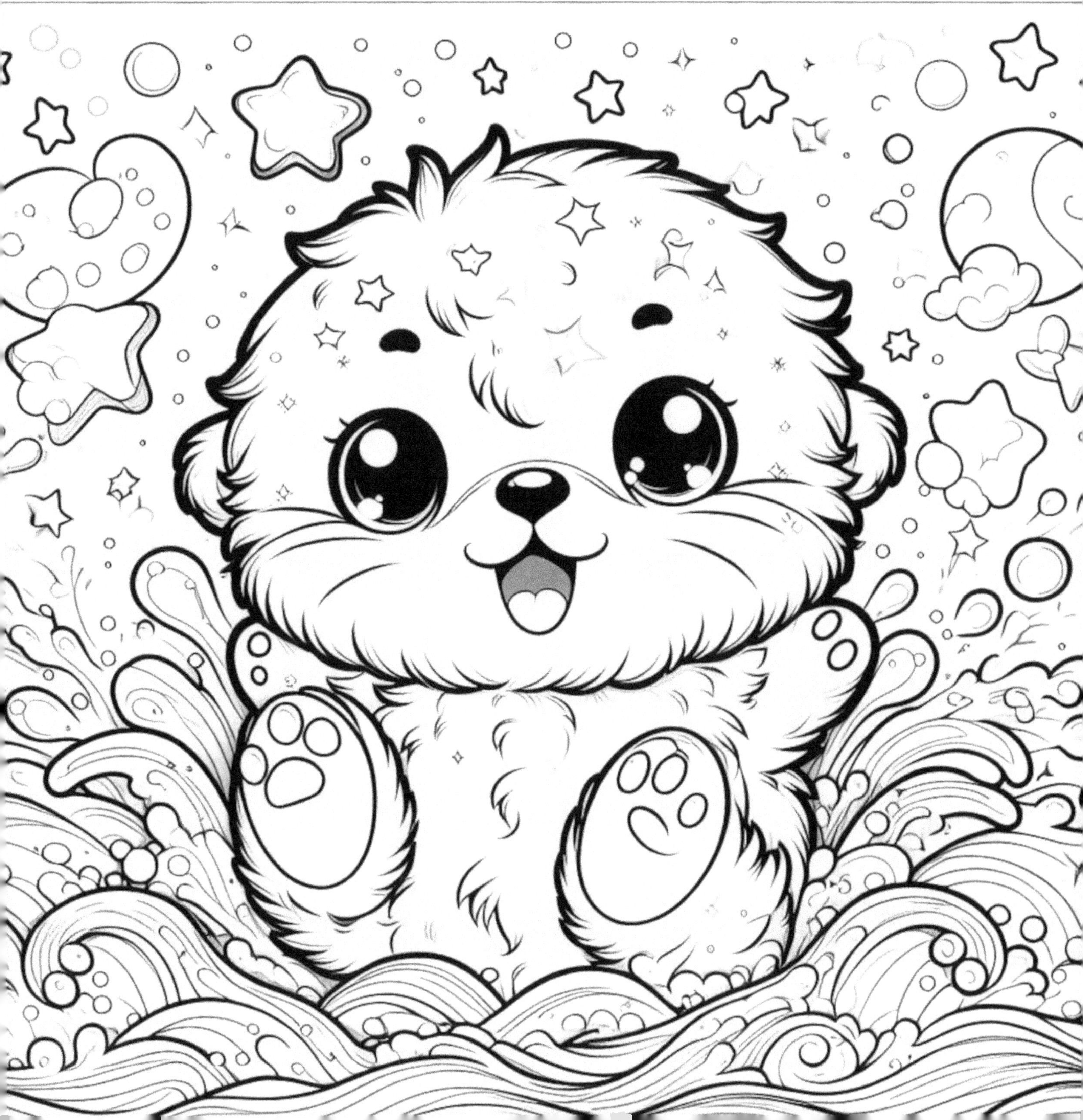

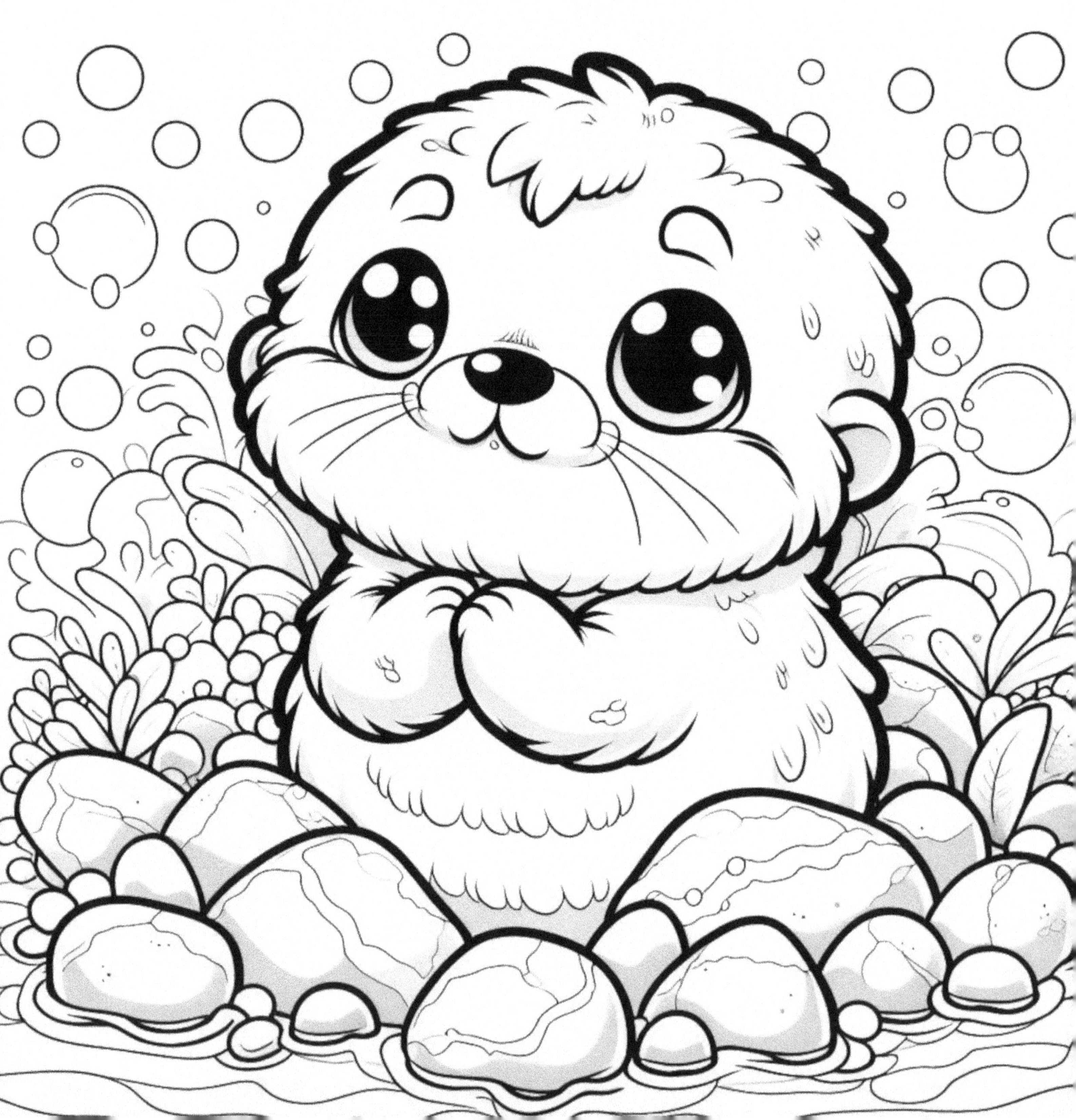

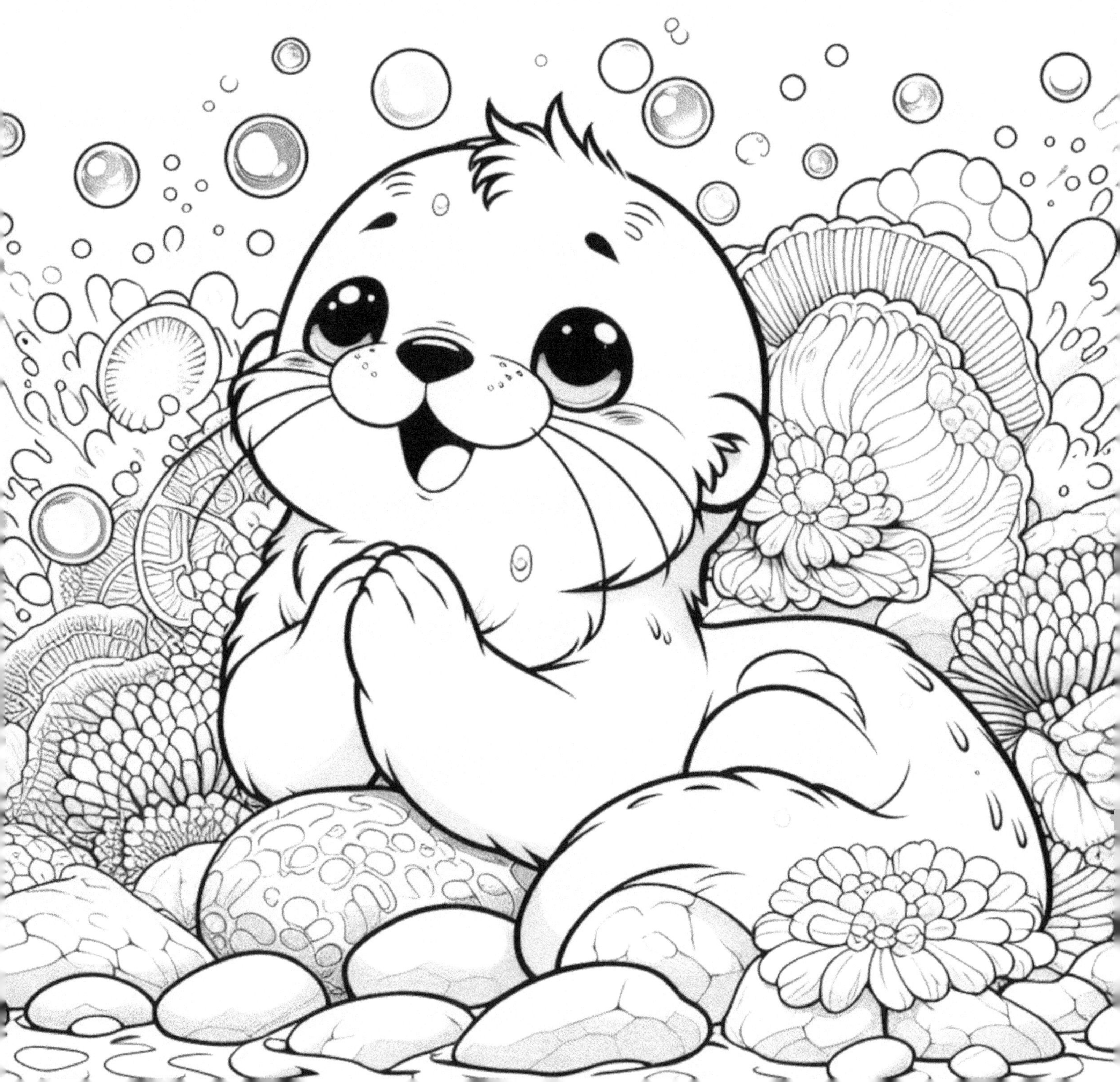

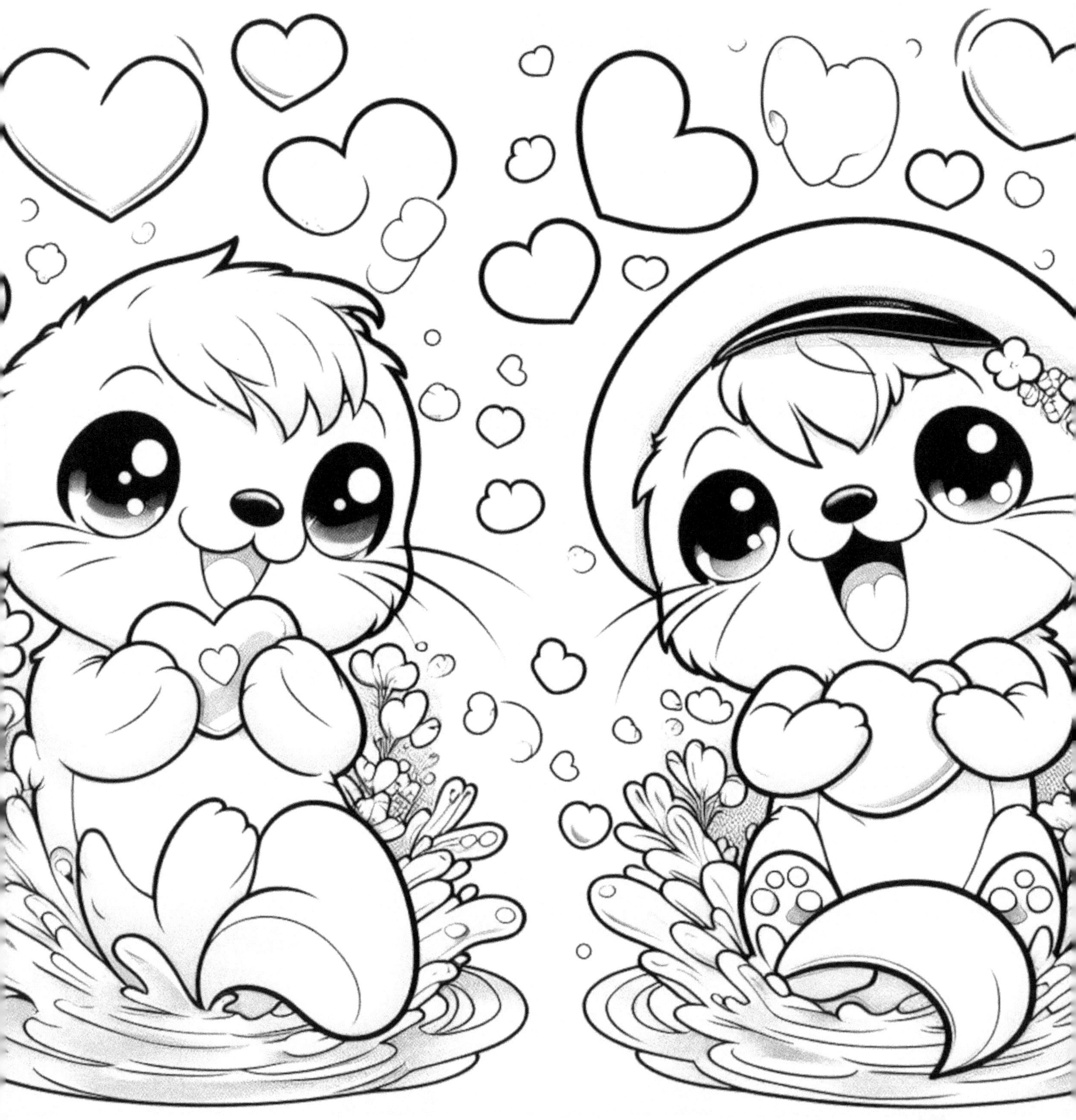

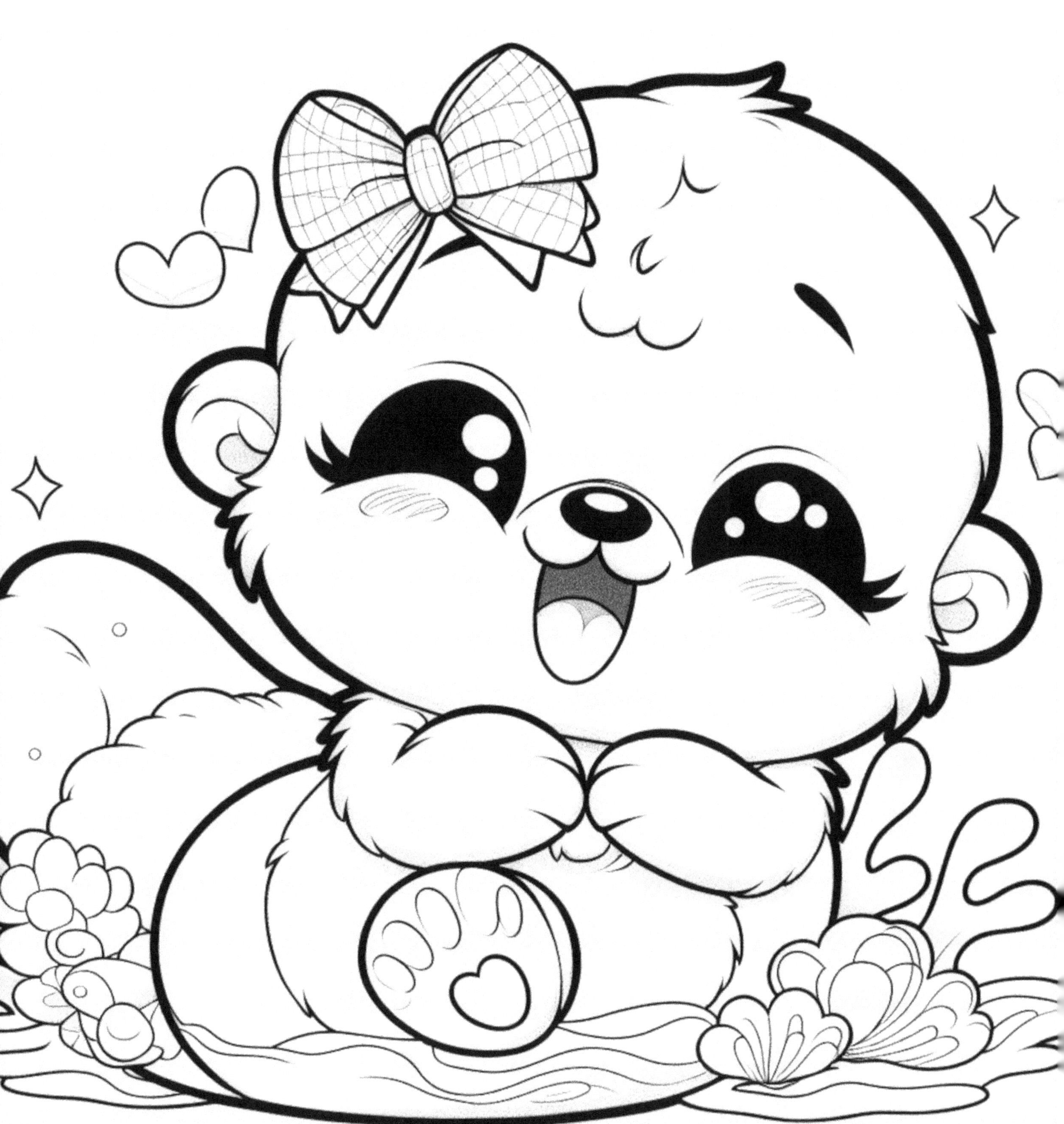

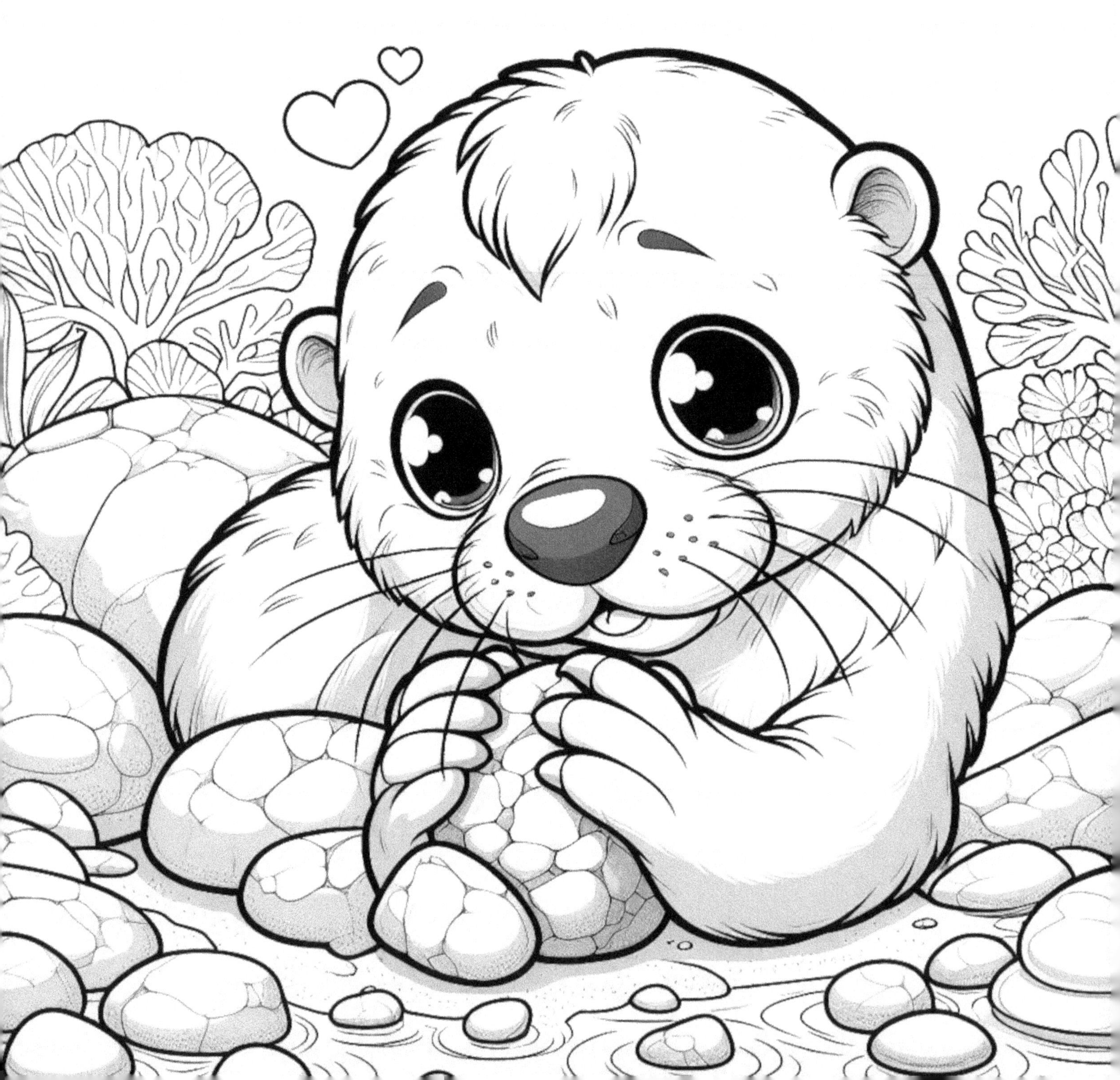

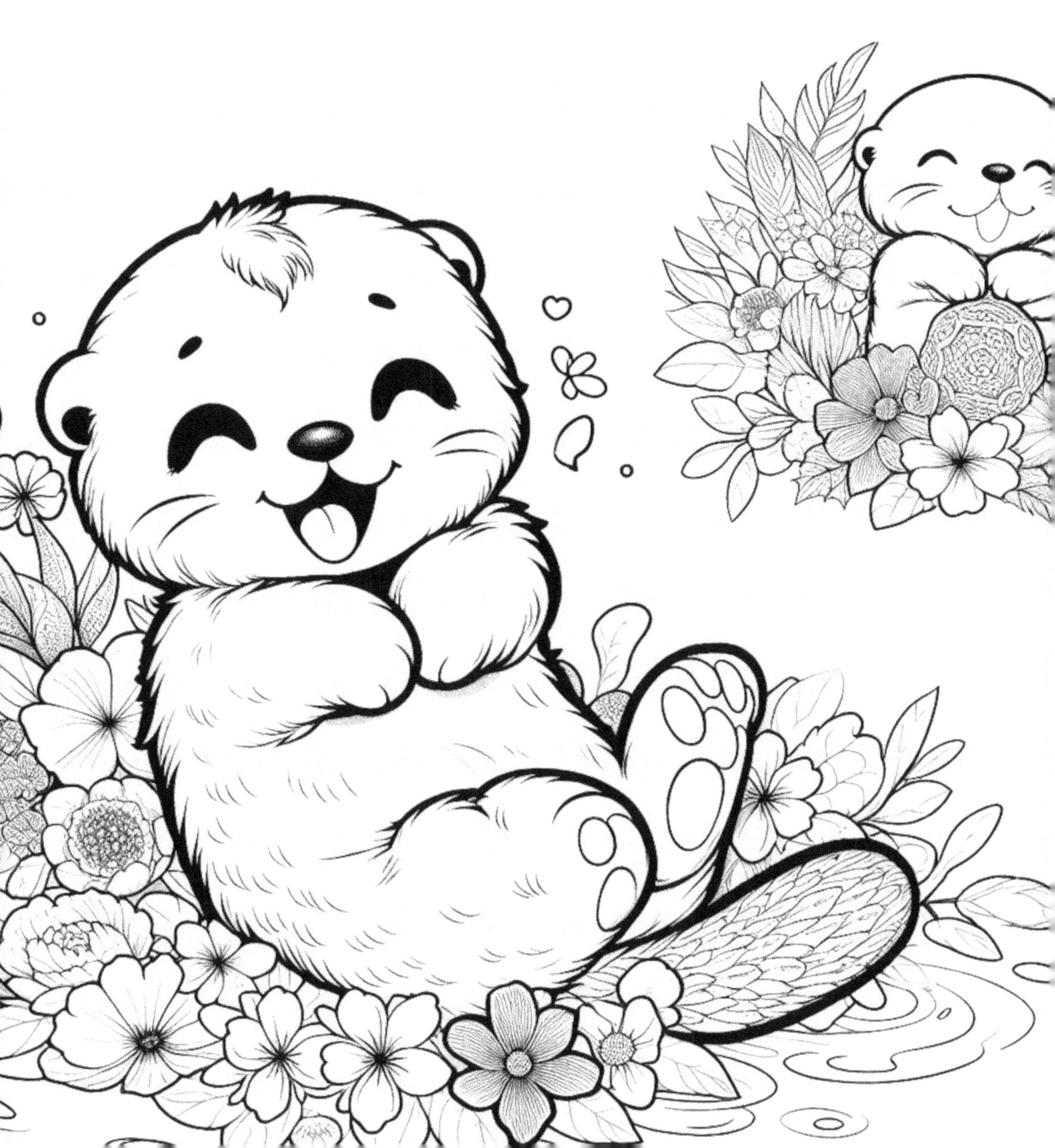

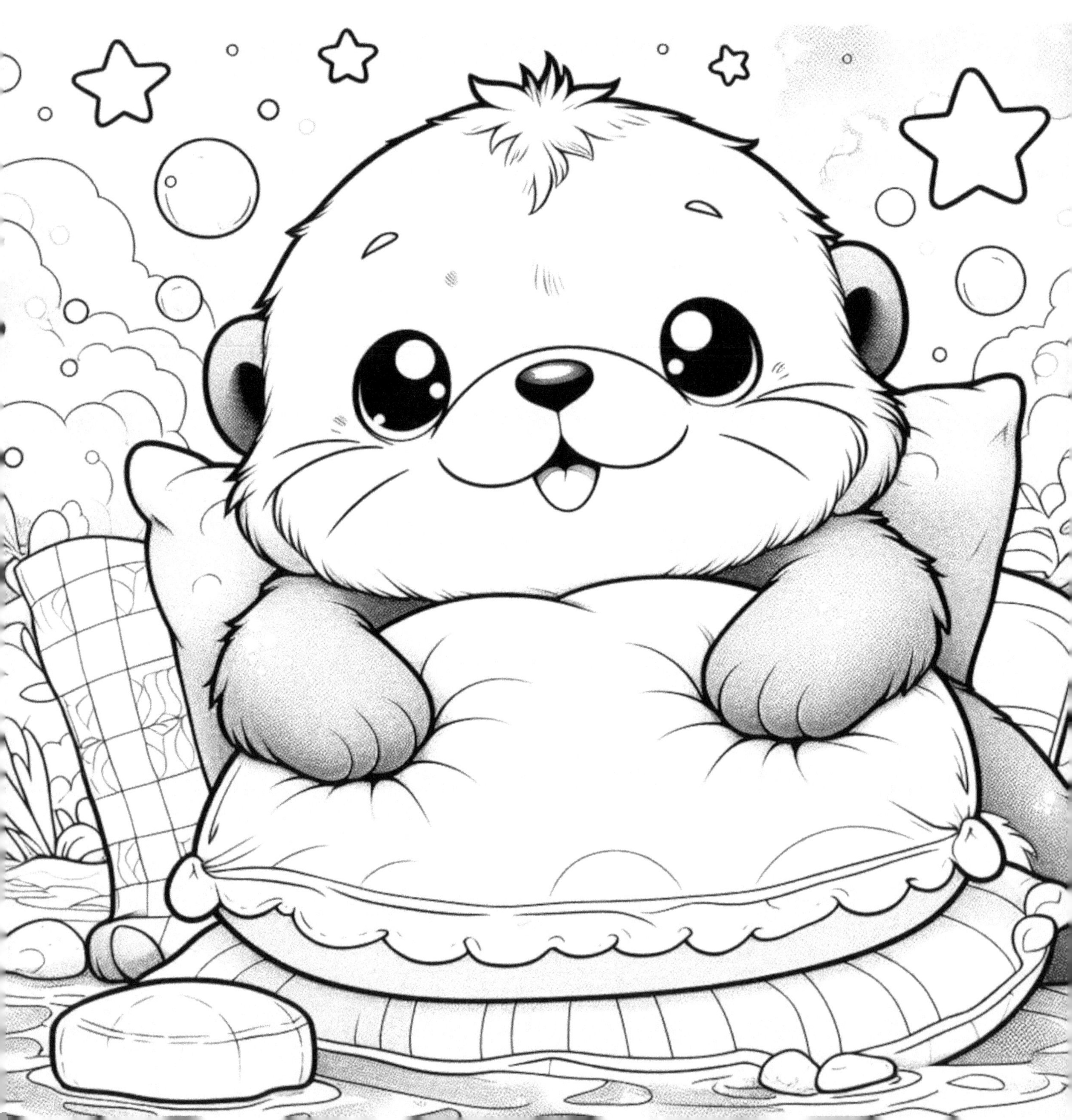

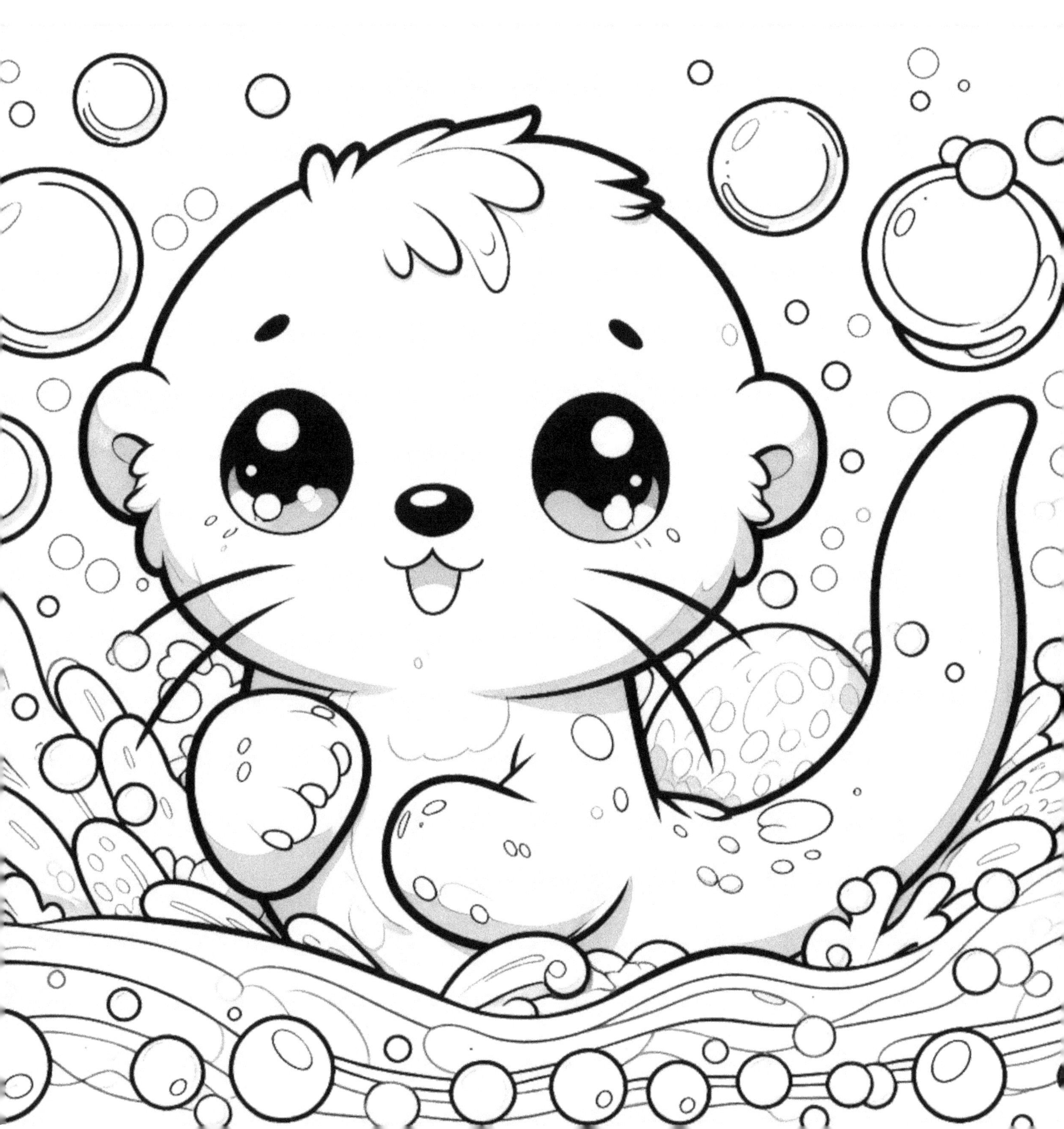

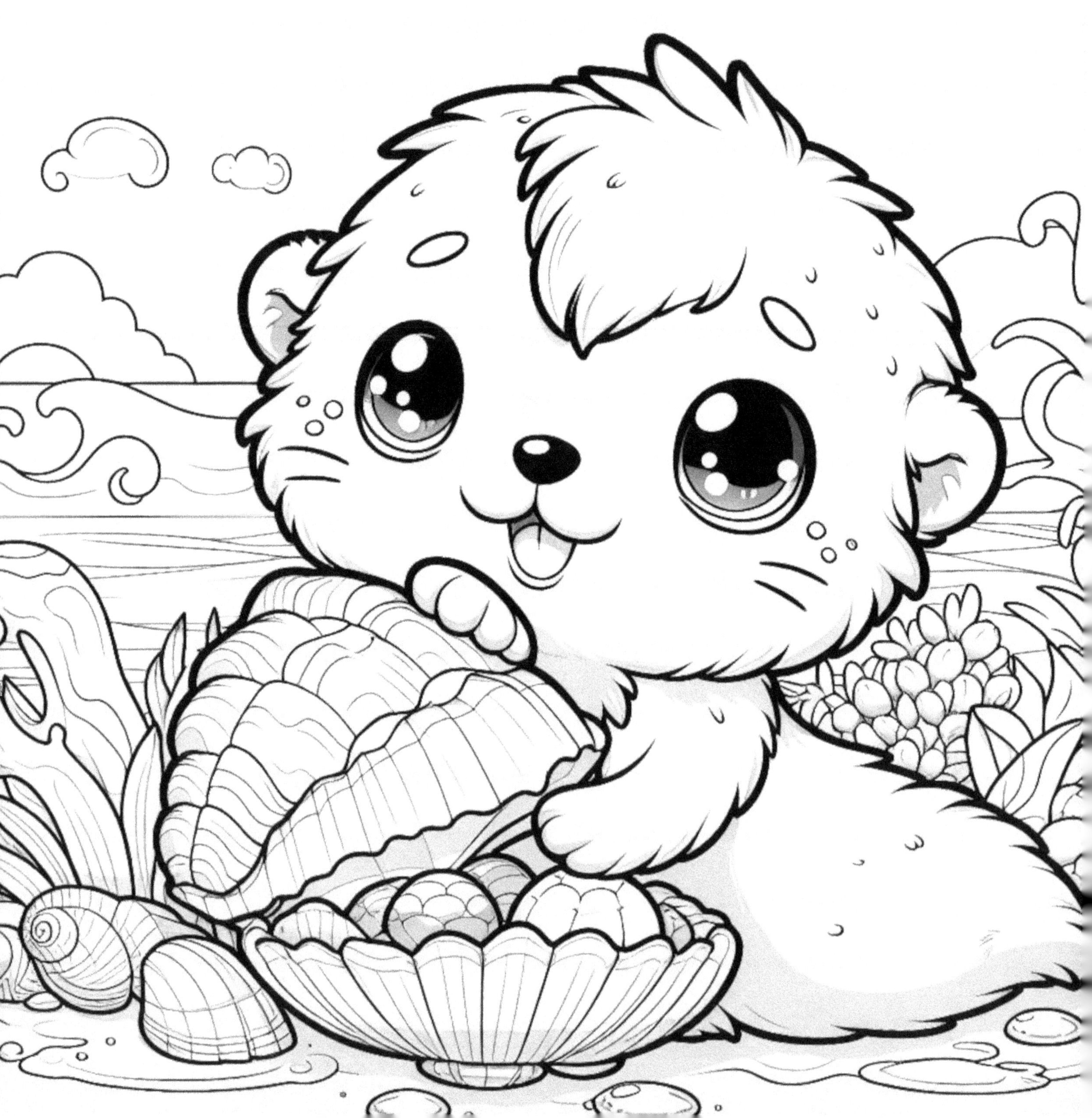

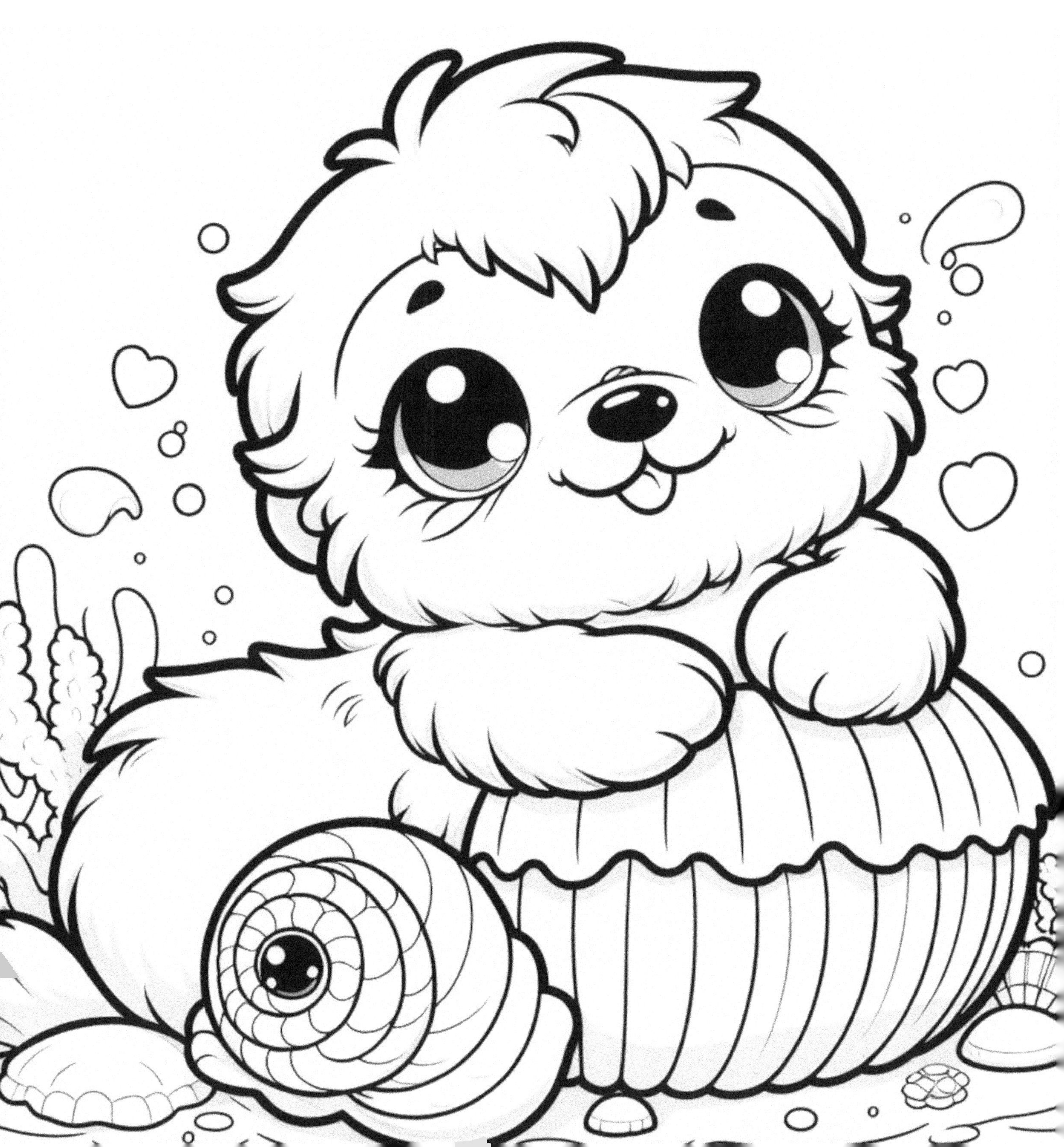

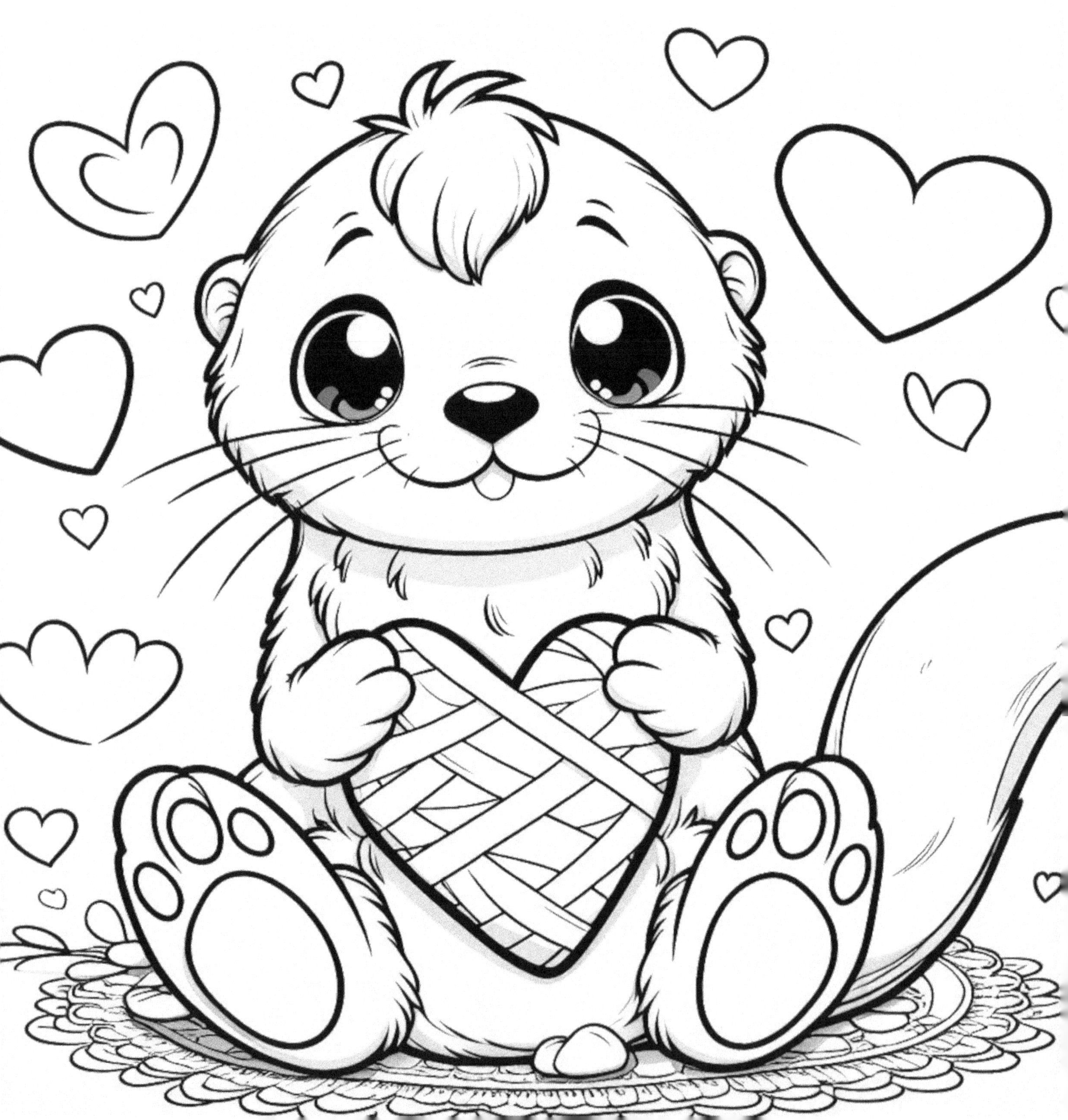

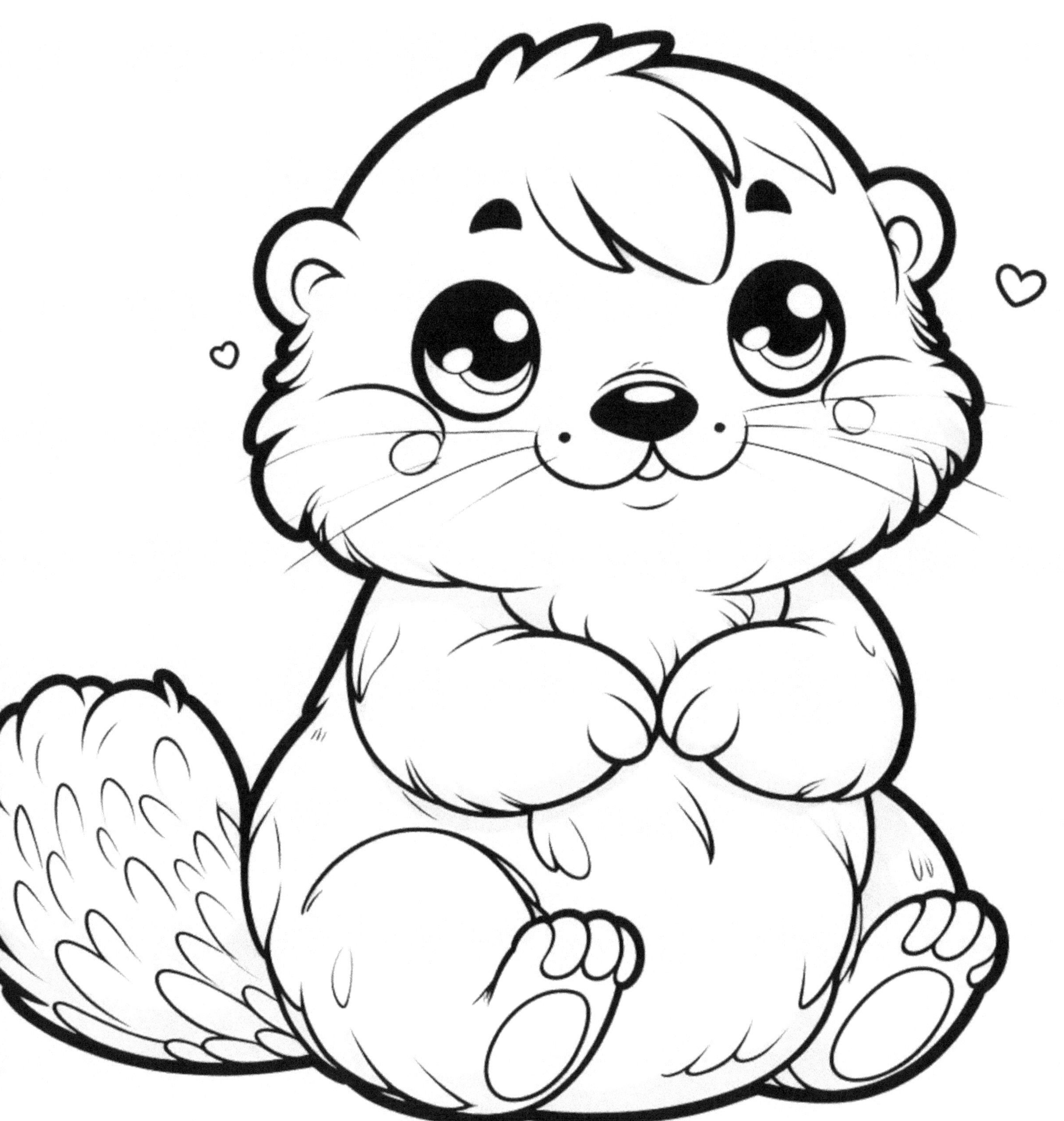

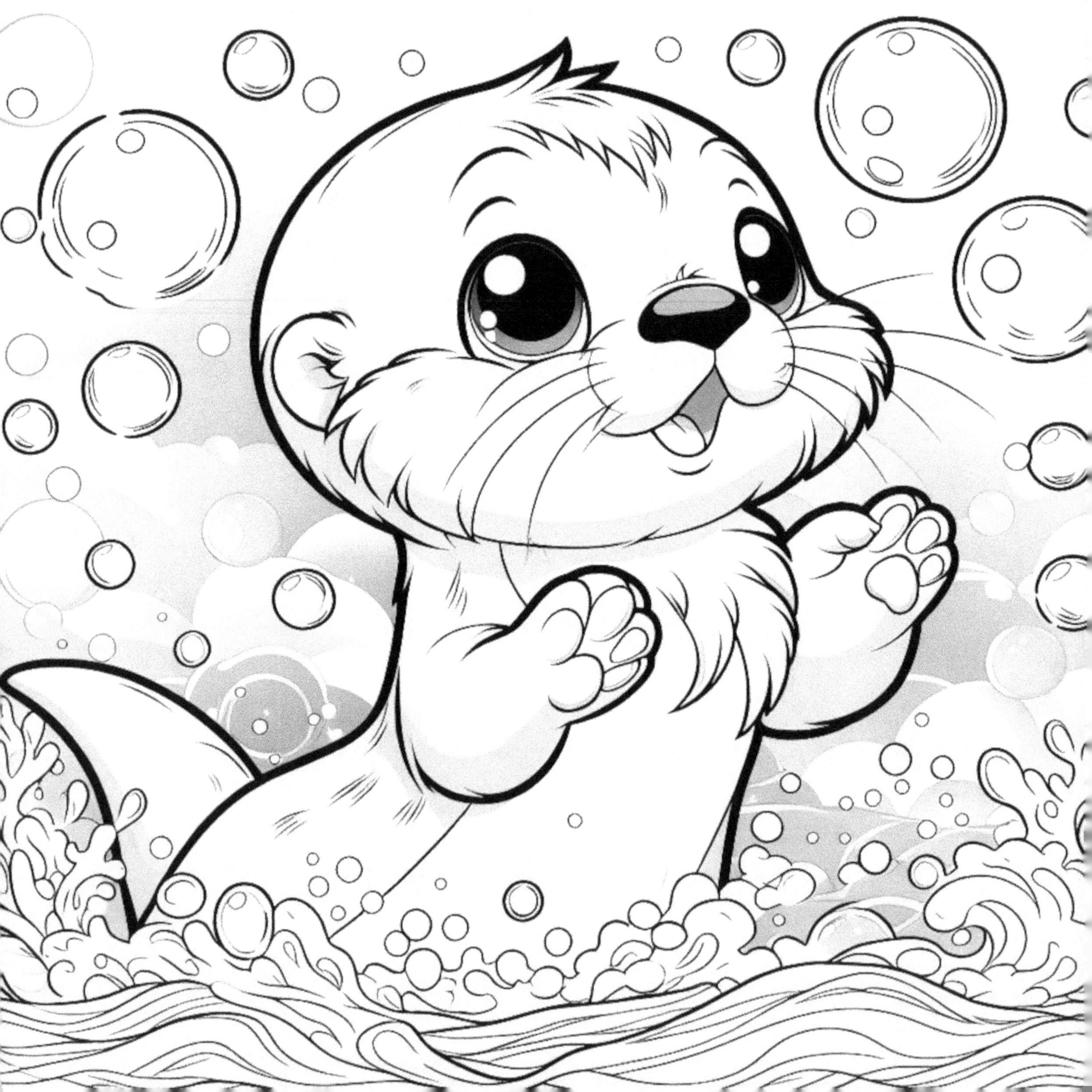

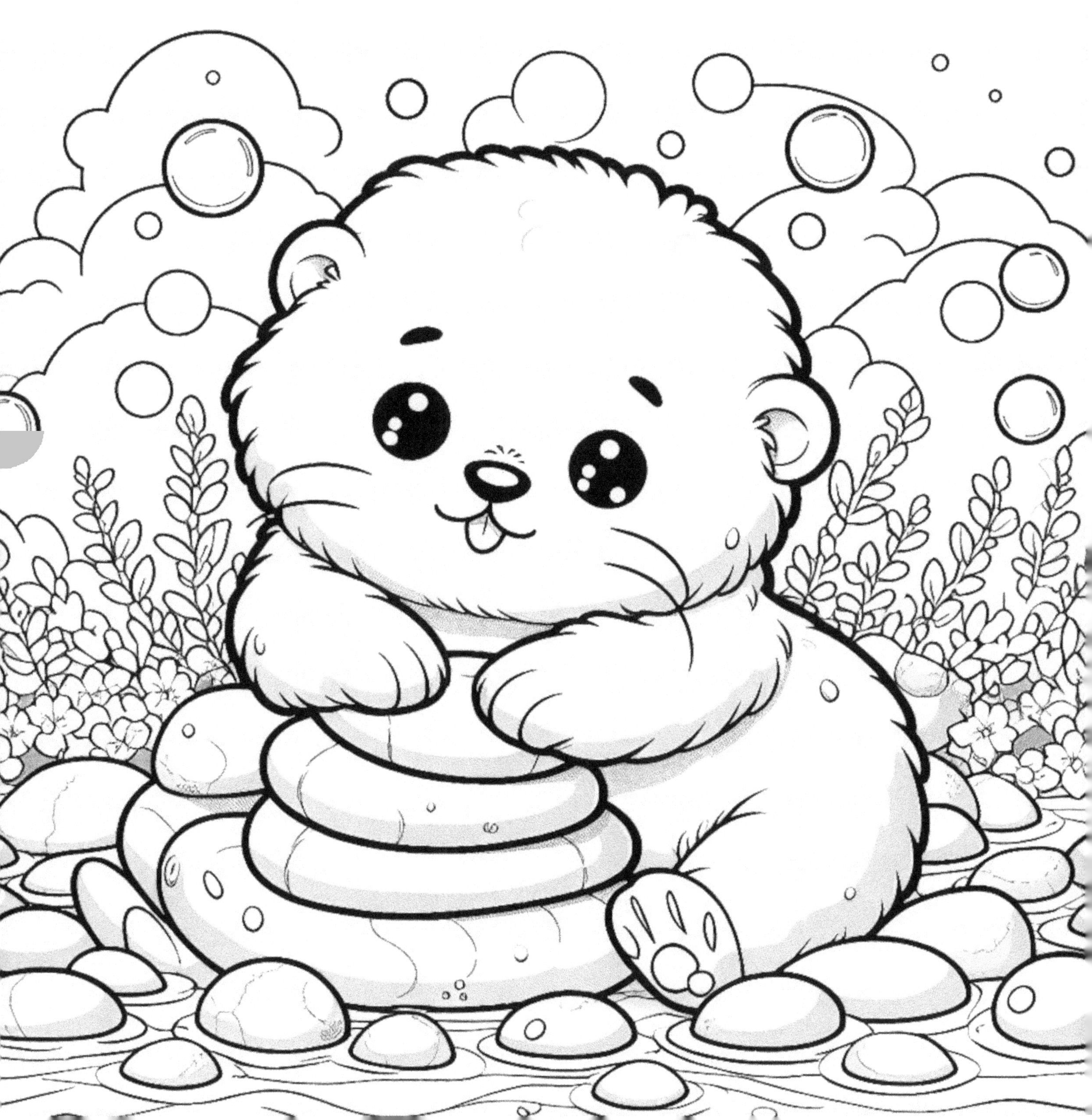

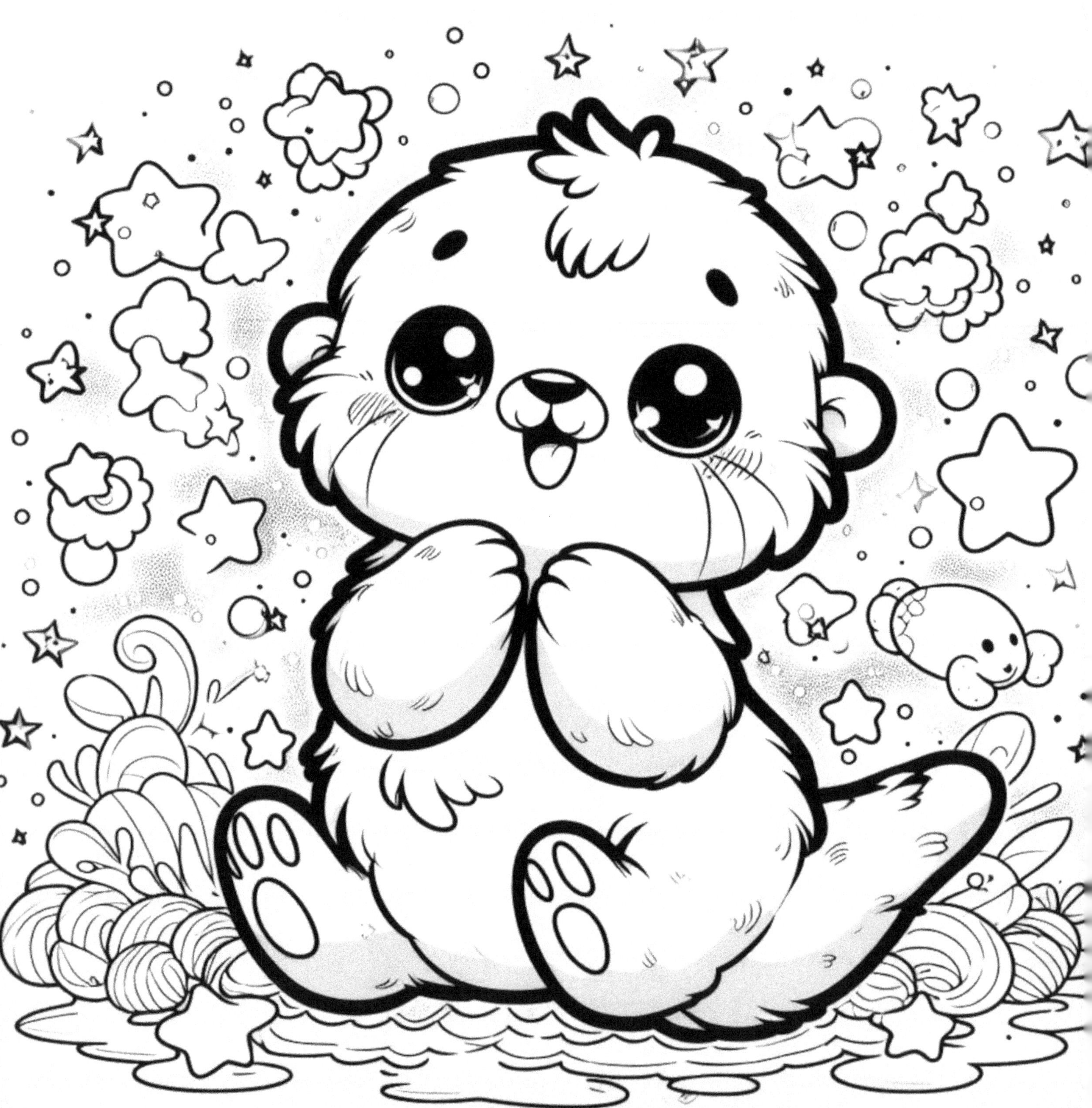

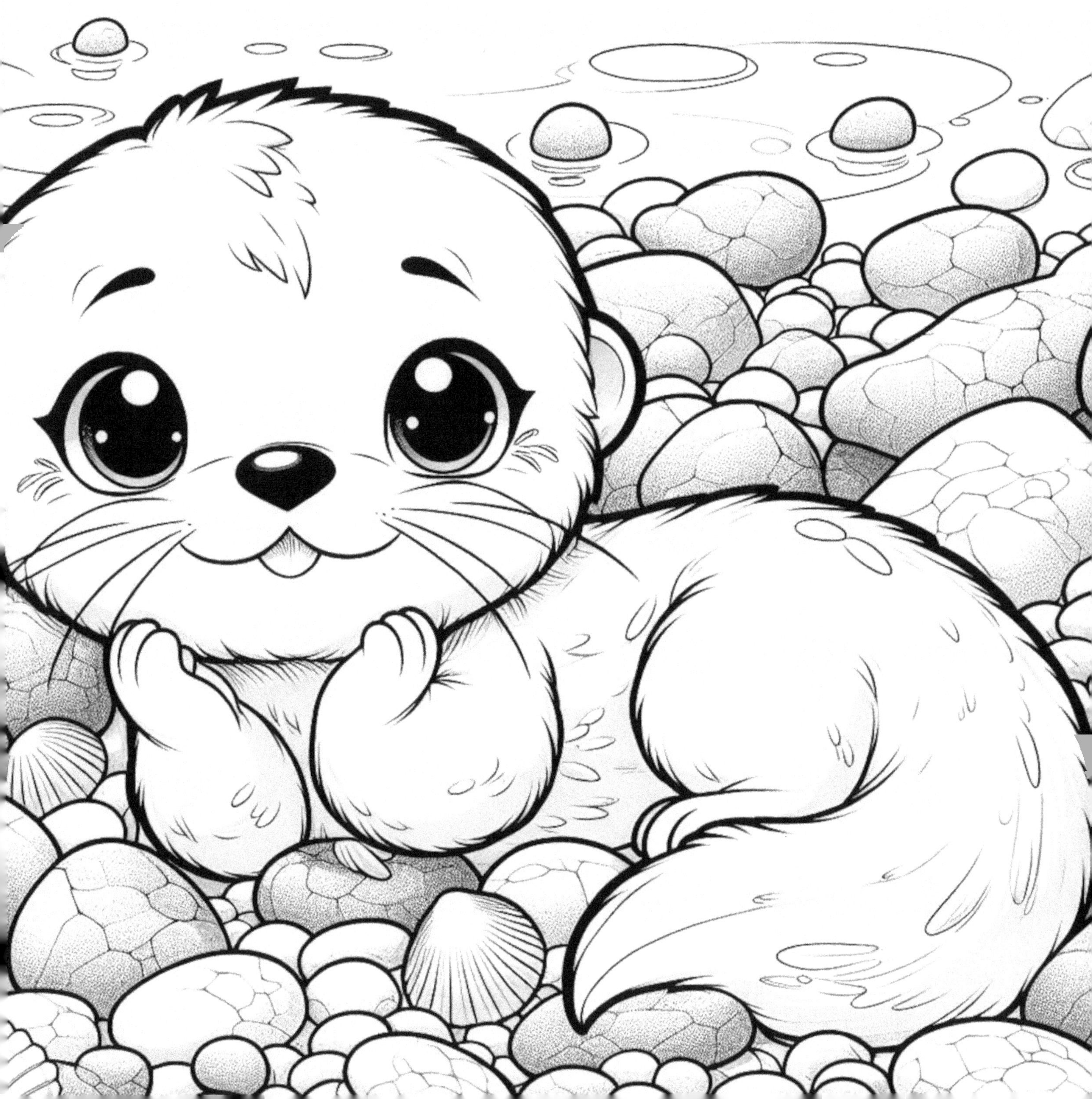

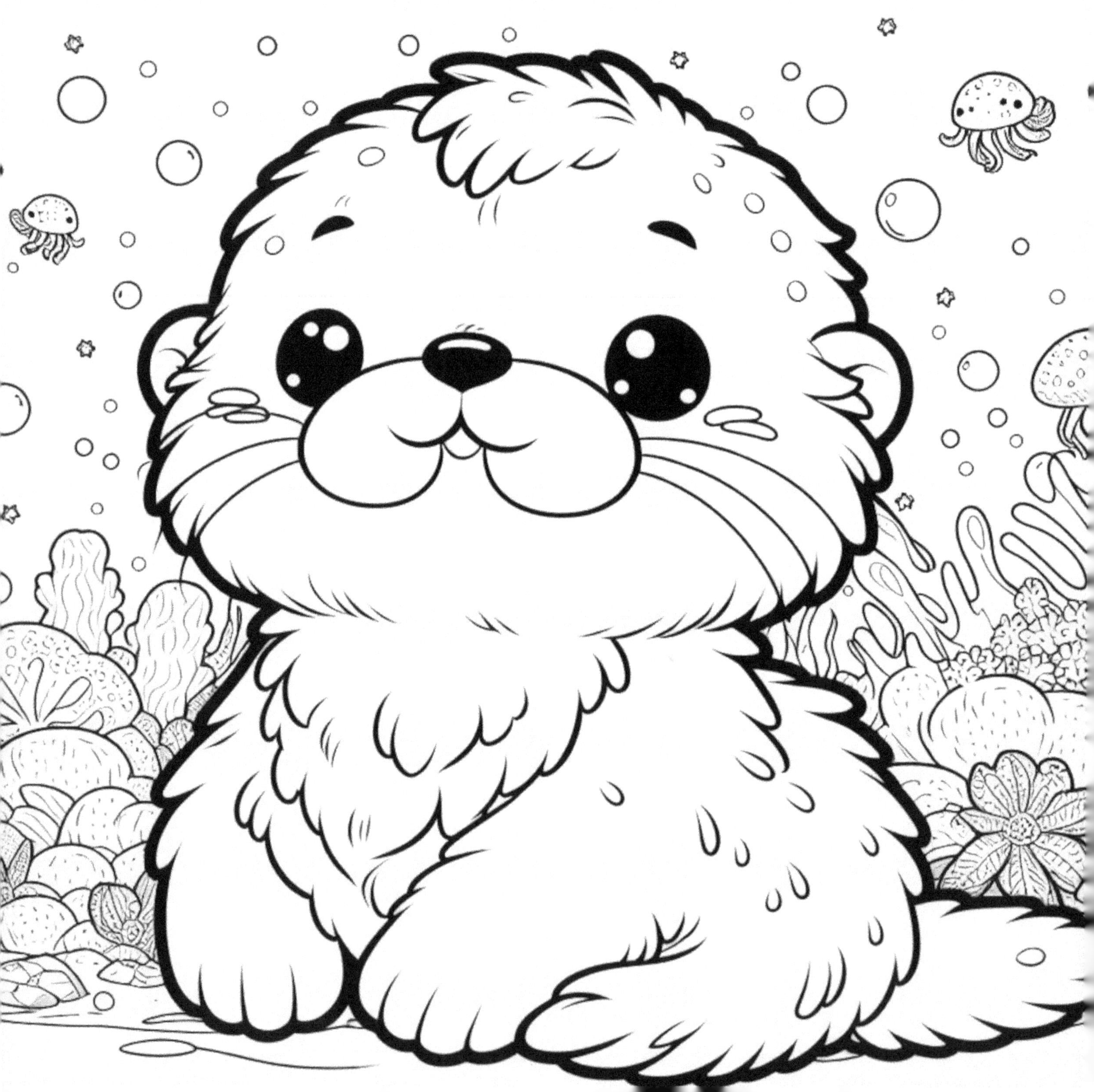

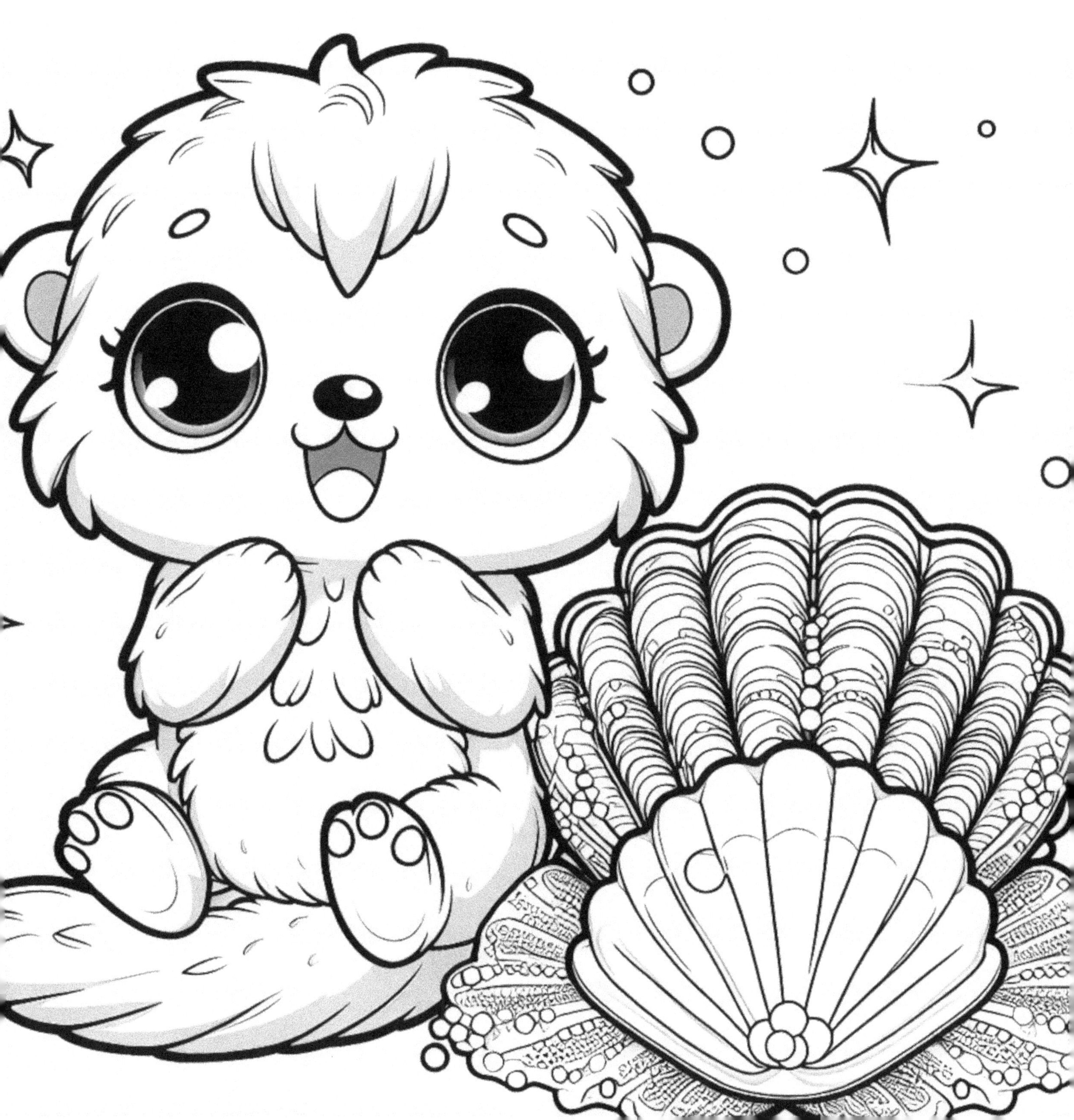

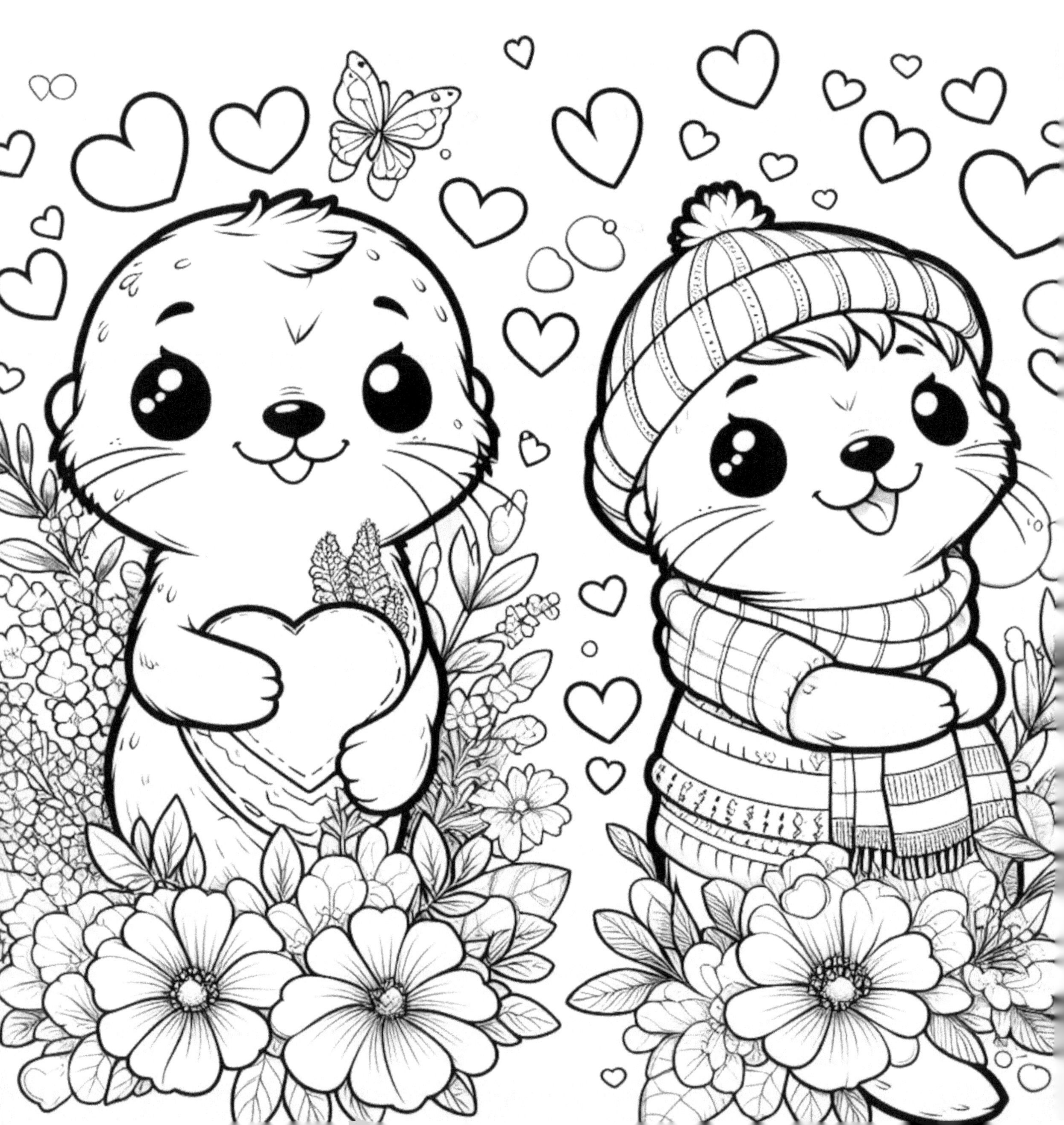